Tilda's Seasonal
Ideas Collection

Tilda's Seasonal Ideas Collection

Tone Finnanger

www.sewandso.co.uk

Contents

Tilda's Spring Ideas

Tilda's Summer Ideas

Tilda's Winter Ideas

Tilda's
SPRING
IDEAS

A Spring Day

Spring is in the air; time for a garden party with good friends and blissful uninterrupted hours in the sewing workroom. It is going to be a great day. There is nothing better than having time to spend on what you like best, your friends and your hobby.

Here you will find two chapters filled with beautiful projects inspired by springtime. In the first chapter, Garden Party, you will find new angels sporting trouser (pant) suits, denim jackets and crochet summer hats, plus gorgeous décor ideas and festive bags. You will also meet Bug, a funny guy who takes care of the party's delicacies; too busy to worry about carbs and calories. The second chapter, Sewing Workshroom, introduces us to a sewing angel inspired by Marilyn Monroe, with a cheeky bright red sewing machine. There are also lovely little storage boxes, cute sewing kits and my personal favourites; the pinwheels – easy is often better.

Happy sewing!

Tone Finnanger

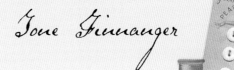

Stuffed Figures

SEWING

Avoid cutting out the parts for a stuffed figure freehand unless absolutely necessary. Fold the fabric double right sides facing, iron and transfer the pattern onto it, see figure A. Sew carefully and evenly along the marked lines, using a stitch length of approximately 1.5mm (⅝in).

CUTTING OUT

Cut out the item with a narrow seam allowance of 3–5mm (⅛– ³⁄₁₆in) along the seams and 8–12mm (⁵⁄₁₆–½in) by the openings. Then cut a notch in the seam allowance where it curves sharply inwards.

REVERSING

Reverse the arms and legs by pushing the blunt end of a wooden stick against the tip of the arm/leg, see figure B. Start closest to the foot/hand and pull the leg/arm down along the wooden stick, see figure C. Continue to pull the leg down the stick until the tip of the foot/hand emerges from the opening. Pull the foot while drawing back the bottom so the leg/arm will be turned inside out, see figure D. Always iron reversed pieces. You can also use the blunt end of a wooden stick to help with stuffing. A good tip is to keep a selection of wooden sticks in different sizes for this purpose.

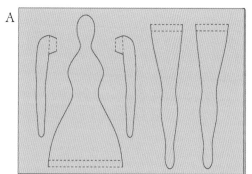

A

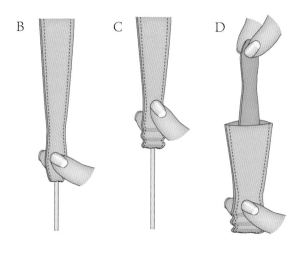

B   C   D

Appliqués

You will find little appliqué signs accompanying some of the models in this book, such as Bug (see pages 12–13) and the Sewing Kit (see pages 30–32). The signs are printed on fabric and can be bought from good Tilda suppliers. They are cut with a 7–10mm (¼– ⅜in) seam allowance. Cut little notches in the seam allowance where it curves sharply before you fold and tack (baste) so the edge around the sign will be as even as possible. The tacking (basting) stitches should be removed when the sign is attached to the model, so it is a good idea to use a bright red thread that is easy to see when you remove it.

Place the sign on the model and stitch around the edges using a thread colour that matches the sign so the stitches are hidden. Remove the tacking (basting) stitches from the seam allowance and iron the sign. Alternatively, the signs can be easily attached using double-sided fusible web, with or without using blanket stitches around the edges.

Face

Push two pins into the head to determine where the eyes should be placed. Remove the pins and fix the eyes into the pinholes using the eye tool from a face kit or a pinhead dipped in paint. Lipstick can be applied using a dry brush to create rosy cheeks when the eyes have dried.

Hair

Insert pins from the forehead down along the middle of the backside of the head. Then insert one pin on either side of the head. Twist hair back and forth between the pins on each side, and divide the hair between the pins in the middle, see figure E. When the head is covered, tack (baste) to attach the hair and remove the pins.

To make a lock of hair, attach the tip of a long "strand of hair" to the head with a long thread. Place the blunt end of a wooden stick against the head where the thread and hair are attached. Make sure the thread is lying against the wooden stick and twist four or five times around the stick and thread, see figure F. Carefully detach the hair from the stick and attach with a couple of stitches, making use of the thread that is already through the locks.

Do not cut thread or hair, but continue to the next lock, see figure G. Continue until you have about eight or nine locks.

If you would like to include a hair bobbin, avoid making locks where this should be attached.

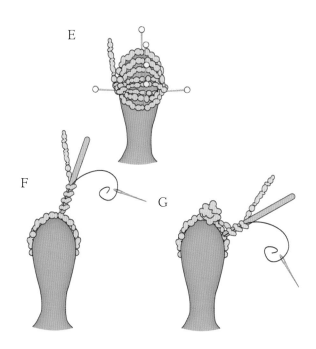

E

F

G

Garden Party

Get ready for the garden party! Gorgeous angels in casual bohemian style with cute butterfly hats and cool denim jackets adorn the picnic tables whilst "Bug" is walking around checking on the food. With cute cupcake garlands, floral party bags and beautiful dog roses decorating the tables, the décor is pleasing to the eye.

Bug

YOU WILL NEED
Fabric for the body
Fabric for the wings
Skin coloured fabric
for the face
Double-sided fusible web
Insert wadding (batting)
Wadding (batting)
Thin steel wire
Buttons

HOW TO MAKE
BODY
Fold the fabric for the body double, right sides facing and trace the figure from the pattern. Sew all the way around and strengthen by sewing a double seam by the neck, under the arms and between the legs.

Cut the figure and cut notches in the seam allowance where the seam turns inwards. Make the reversing opening through one of the fabric layers as marked in the pattern, see figure A. Reverse the figure, using a flower stick or similar to reverse the arms and legs more easily, then iron the figure.

Stuff the figure firmly using wadding (batting) to achieve a nice shape. Close the opening using tacking (basting) stitches.

Iron double-sided fusible web against a piece of the skin fabric and pull off the paper. Trace and cut the face from the pattern and iron it to the head.

Sew blanket stitches around the face if you wish.

COLLAR
Cut a strip of fabric to measure 30 × 4cm (12 × 1½in), adding a seam allowance. Iron in the seam allowances and fold the strip in half to measure 30 × 2cm (12 × ¾in).

Sew with large stitches along the open edge and pucker the stitching to create a clown collar effect.

Attach the collar around the neck using tacking (basting) stitches.

WINGS AND ANTENNAE
Fold the fabric for the wings double, right sides facing and place insert wadding (batting) underneath. Trace and sew around the wings. Cut and make a reverse opening through one of the layers as marked in the pattern, reverse and iron. Glue or tack (baste) on the wings so the reverse opening on the wings is turning in towards the reverse opening at the back.

Cut a small piece of thin steel wire to 30cm (12in). Push a doll needle or similar through the top of the head to create an opening, see figure B, then carefully insert the steel wire. Thread a button onto both ends of the steel wire. Decide a suitable length for the antennae before you twist the wire around itself underneath the button and cut the ends.

Make a face as described on page 9.

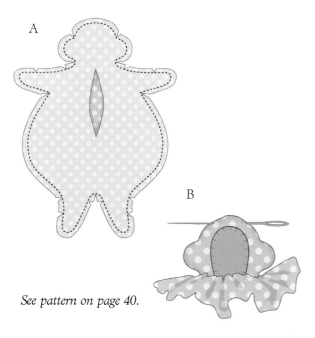

A

B

See pattern on page 40.

Springtime Bags

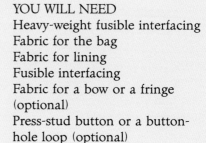

HOW TO MAKE

BAG

Note that the pattern is divided in two pieces to fit the pattern page. Put the pieces together by lining up points A and B. Double the pattern to make both sides of the bag and mark with a folding edge.

Cut a piece of iron-on fusible interfacing equal to the whole pattern, lid included. Add a seam allowance around the bag, but not around the lid. Also cut a piece that equals the whole bag without the lid, adding a seam allowance around the whole bag except along the top edge.

Iron the fusible interfacing piece against the wrong side of the fabric you wish to use. Cut right next to the seam allowance at the fusible interfacing side around the bag, adding some extra seam allowance around the lid. Cut notches in the seam allowance around the lid.

Cut strips of double-sided fusible web, pull the adhesive from the paper and place the strips between the seam allowance when ironing, see figure A.

Repeat this method on the part without the lid, and iron in some extra seam allowance using iron-on double-sided fusible web along the top edge.

Place the two parts right sides facing and stitch together on each side and at the bottom, see figure B.

Fold opposite so the seams meet and stitch up the openings on each side to create a base, see figure C.

LINING

Sew the lining fabric in the same way as for the bag, but iron and tack (baste) the seam allowance around the lid and along the edge without double-sided fusible web.

Place the lining inside the bag so the wrong side of the lining is against the fusible interfacing. Sew around the lid and along the edge, see figure D. Iron the bag and lid into position.

YOU WILL NEED
Heavy-weight fusible interfacing
Fabric for the bag
Fabric for lining
Fusible interfacing
Fabric for a bow or a fringe (optional)
Press-stud button or a button-hole loop (optional)

BOW

Note that the pattern for the bow is marked with a folding edge and should be doubled. Fold the fabric for the bow right sides facing and trace the bow. Sew around, leaving a reverse opening in the seam, then cut, reverse and iron. Fold the bow, see figure E.

Cut a strip of fabric to 1.5cm (⅝in) plus seam allowance, fold in the seam allowance and tighten the fabric strip around the bow. Attach to the bag.

FRINGE

Tear a fabric strip to 3cm (1⅛in) × the fabric width, seam allowance included. Using a sewing machine, sew a 6mm (¼in) seam along one of the edges without attaching the thread. Pucker by pulling the thread until the strip ruffles to equal the perimeter of the lid.

Sew the strip to the underside of the lid so about 2cm (¾in) will show outside the edge. Remove loose threads. Use a press-stud button or a loop for the closing mechanism of the bag. Attach the press-stud button as described in the manufacturer's instructions.

See pattern on page 41.

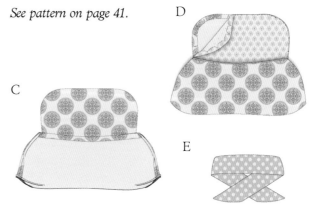

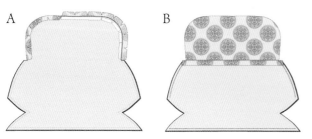

Garden Party Angels

HOW TO MAKE

BODY

Note that the patterns for the body and legs are divided to fit the pattern page. Put the pieces together by lining up points A and B. Fold the skin fabric right sides facing and trace a body, two arms and two legs. Sew around all the parts.

Cut out all of the parts and cut notches in the seam allowance where the seams are turning inwards.

Reverse and iron the parts, then iron in the seam allowance on the body and arms.

Stuff the bottom part of the leg with wadding (batting) up to the thin, dotted line in the pattern. Sew a seam across the "knee" before you stuff the rest of the leg, see figure A.

Stuff the body and arms. Place the legs inside the body and tack (baste), see figure B. The arms should be attached a little behind the chest so they are positioned leaning slightly back from the shoulders and closer to the body, see figure C.

TROUSER (PANT) SUIT

Cut a piece of fabric to measure 20 × 10cm (8 × 4in) for the top, adding a seam allowance. Fold the fabric double, right sides facing, to become 20 × 5cm (8 × 2in) broad, and sew along the open long side.

YOU WILL NEED

Fabric for the body
Fabric for the trouser (pant) suit
Fabric for the wings
Thin denim fabric
Tilda hair or similar
Wadding (batting)
White pearls 3–4mm (⅛–⁵⁄₃₂in)
Embroidery yarn or thin crochet yarn

Reverse and iron the top. Sew a seam across the middle and pucker, see figure D.

Attach the top so the puckered area is at the neck, and the ends overlap in front. Attach with a few stitches, see figure E.

See patterns on pages 42–45.

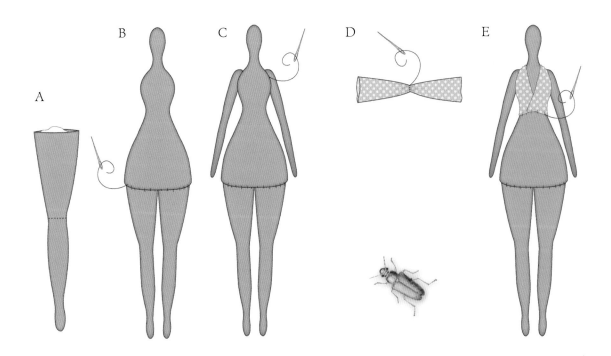

Note that the trousers pattern is divided to fit the pattern page. Place the parts together by lining up points A and B. The pattern is marked with a folding edge and should be doubled.

Cut two trouser parts, place them right sides facing and stitch up, see figure F. Fold the trousers opposite so the seams are lying over and under each other, and stitch up the legs, see figure G.

Iron in the seam allowance by the openings for the legs then dress the trousers onto the angel. The trousers should be attached fairly high up on the waist. Fold two tucks in the front and two at the back and attach with tacking (basting) stitches. Tack (baste) around the edge of each opening and pucker the legs together around the angel's leg, see figure H.

DENIM JACKET

It is important to use a thin denim fabric for this jacket as it is very detailed. Here we have used Tilda denim fabric with white sewing thread for an authentic finishing touch.

Cut out a piece of fabric large enough for four pockets, fold twice and trace one of the two pockets from the pattern. Sew around, cut out, reverse and iron the pockets.

Cut out two front parts and one back part. Place the pockets on each front part and stitch in place, see figure I. Fold the pockets down and sew a seam to hold them in place, see figure J.

Fold the fabric for the collar twice, trace the collar from the pattern and sew around, see figure K. Cut, reverse and iron the collar. Sew a seam 3mm (⅛in) inside the edge with white sewing thread, see figure L.

Cut out two sleeves from the pattern. Sew the front pieces to the back piece by the shoulders and sew a sleeve onto each side, see figure M.

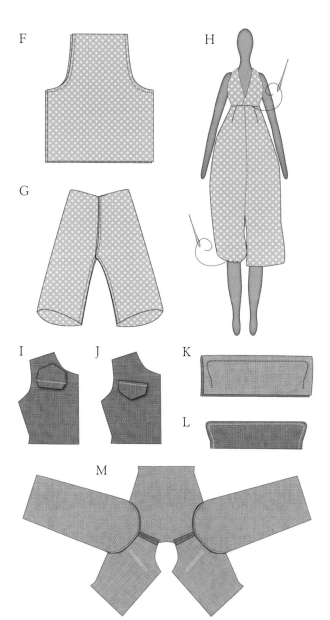

Fold up the seam allowance at the bottom of each sleeve and sew around. Fold the jacket right sides facing and stitch up underneath the sleeves on each side of the jacket, see figure N.

Cut a notch in the seam allowance close to the seam underneath the sleeves and in the curved seam allowance. This will avoid a stretch between the sleeves and shoulders when reversing. Iron the jacket.

Place the collar against the right side of the jacket, positioning the middle of the collar against the middle of the backside. Sew the collar to the jacket, see figure O. Fold and iron the collar upwards, so the seam is facing the inside of the jacket, before you fold the upper part of the collar down.

Iron in the seam allowance on each side by the openings at the front of the jacket and sew. Fold and iron in the seam allowance along the edge at the bottom of the jacket and sew, see figure P.

Sew little pearls as buttons on the pockets along the opening, see picture opposite. To make the decorative dog rose, see page 23.

Dress the jacket onto the figure. For the jacket to fit nicely, you can tack (baste) it to the figure where necessary.

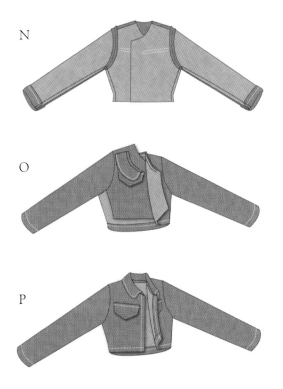

N

O

P

WINGS

Fold the fabric twice and trace the wings from the pattern. Sew around the wings, see figure Q. Reverse and iron the wings and sew the seams as marked in the pattern, see figure R. Stuff the wings by using a wooden stick and stitch up the opening, then tack (baste) the wings to the figure.

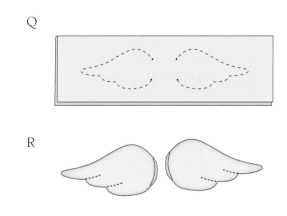

Q

R

CROCHET SUMMER HAT

If you do not wish to crochet a hat, make hair as described on page 9.

Embroidery yarn and a crochet hook number 2 are used to make these small, quick-to-make hats. Try to ensure that the threads do not separate. You can alternatively use thin crochet yarn, but you must measure the head first to size the hat correctly.

Make 24 ch (chain stitches) and make a circle.
1st round: Start the round with 1 ch and make 23 sc (single crochets). Finish with 1 sl st (slip stitch) in the 1st ch.
2nd round: Start the round with 2 ch – 1 dc (double crochet). Then crochet 23 dc. Finish with 1 sl st in 2nd ch.
3rd round: Start the round with 2 ch – 1 dc (double crochets). Crochet 23 dc. Finish with 1 sl st in 2nd ch.
4th round: Start the round with 2 ch – 1 dc. Crochet 1 dc, skip 1 dc, crochet 2 dc, skip 1 dc, and continue throughout the round.
Finish by pulling the yarn through the top crochet stitches and attach.

Place a few "strands of hair" inside the hat before you place it on the head to prevent the scalp from showing through the stitches. Make two large balls of hair and attach to each side of the head with pins before you tack (baste) in place.

Make face as described on page 9.

Dog Roses

YOU WILL NEED
Fabric for the rose petals
Pearls

HOW TO MAKE

Use 3 and 4mm (⅛ and ⁵⁄₃₂in) pearls for the small dog roses and 3 and 5mm (⅛ and ³⁄₁₆in) pearls for the larger ones.

Trace and cut petals from the pattern without adding a seam allowance. You will need five petals to make one flower.

Pull out a few loose threads around the edge of the flower petals to create a frayed fringe edge. Iron every petal folded in half wrong sides facing. Sew in the fold through a petal with large stitches and continue with the next petal, see figure A.

When you have finished, use the same thread to sew through all the petals, puckering them together carefully. Sew several rounds, pulling the thread gradually more tightly until the opening in the middle of the flower is as small as possible, see figure B. Stitch on the pearls alternating between attaching the large and small pearls to the folds around the edge.

The flowers can be used to decorate many projects, from brightening up dolls' clothing (see picture opposite) to embellishing a box or lamp shade (see page 33).

See pattern on page 47.

A

B

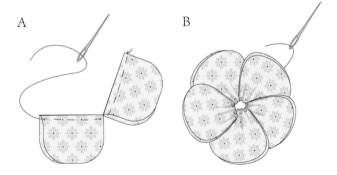

Gift Bags

HOW TO MAKE

Trace the pattern for the bag twice beside each other and finish with the flap to create a net for the box, see figure A.

Cut out the bag without including a seam allowance. Use a utility knife and ruler to mark all the folds indicated with a dotted line in the pattern.

Fold the top edge down, the flaps for the bottom up, and the mid folds on each short side together with the adhesive flap inwards, see figure B. Apply paper adhesive to the adhesive flap and glue the bag together, then glue the flaps at the bottom together.

Make holes in the bag for the handles using a belt punch or similar and tie the strings to the bag.

See pattern on page 46.

See pattern on page 46.

YOU WILL NEED
Stiff scrapbook paper
Paper adhesive (an adhesive roller is recommended)
String for the handle
Utility knife
Ruler

A

B

Cupcake Garland

I'm always thinking about easy seasonal decoration ideas and was very happy when I came up with this pretty cupcake garland. With a great selection of cupcake liners available in a wide range of colours, they are a simple but effective material for this quick-to-make garland. Use a variety of liners and patterns or stick to just one type for a simpler design.

HOW TO MAKE
Flatten the cupcake liners and fold them twice wrong sides facing. Fold out again and apply a line of adhesive next to the fold on one side. Place the string in the central fold then fold the liner in half to stick in place. Repeat with your desired number of cupcake liners to create your garland.

YOU WILL NEED
String
Cupcake liners
Adhesive (an adhesive roller is recommended)

Sewing Workroom

If you have a great passion for needlework, nothing can compare with blissful undisturbed hours in the sewing workroom, by the dining table or wherever you have made room for your hobby. Here you will find ideas for sewing fanatics, including pin cushions, cute sewing kits and last but not least, a cheeky little sewing angel with a bright red sewing machine.

Pinwheels

HOW TO MAKE

Cut out a strip of fabric measuring 35 × 12.5cm (13¾ × 4⅞in), adding a seam allowance. Cut a strip of iron-on heavy-weight fusible interfacing measuring 35 × 2.5cm (13¾ × 1in), only adding a seam allowance to each short side so it remains 2.5cm (1in) wide.

Place the interfacing strip in the middle of the wrong side of the fabric strip with the adhesive side down. Iron and sew a seam along each long side of the interfacing strip, about 2mm (³⁄₃₂in) from the edge.

Iron in the seam allowance along each long side of the fabric strip and fold the strip double, right sides facing. Stitch up the open side, see figure A and reverse so the right side is facing out.

Use embroidery yarn to sew around one of the edges and pucker to create the base of the pinwheel. Cut out a cardboard circle equal to the large circle in the pattern and push the cardboard down towards the bottom inside the pinwheel, see figure B.

Sew around the other edge. Stuff the pinwheel firmly with wadding (batting) before you pucker it together and attach the thread, see figure C. Steam with the iron to press the pinwheel into a flatter shape.

Fold a piece of fabric that is big enough for the smaller circle in the pattern twice right sides facing. Trace and sew around the circle. Cut out the circle and make a reversing opening through one of the layers. Reverse and iron.

YOU WILL NEED
Fabric for the wheel
Fabric for the circle
Heavy-weight fusible interfacing with an adhesive side
Strong cardboard
Embroidery yarn
Wadding (batting)

Place the circle in the middle of the pinwheel on the opposite side to the cardboard base. Tack (baste) the circle using the same colour embroidery yarn to create invisible stitches.

Fold a ribbon in half and tack (baste) it to the underside of the pinwheel to act as a hanger.

See pattern on page 44.

A

B

C

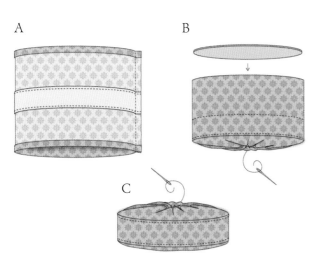

Sewing Kit

HOW TO MAKE

Trace and cut out a piece of iron-on heavy-weight fusible interfacing measuring 42 × 14cm (16½ × 5½in) without a seam allowance. Use a ruler to ensure that the corners are straight. Use a small bobbin or coin to draw a smooth curve in each corner and cut out. Make another piece the same way, but this should be 3mm (⅛in) shorter in length and height, i.e. 41.7 × 13.7cm (16⅜ × 5⅜in).

The largest piece will be the outside of the sewing kit. Place it with the adhesive side down towards the wrong side of your desired fabric and iron to attach the interfacing to the fabric.

Cut around the fabric, leaving a minimum of 1cm (⅜in) seam allowance of fabric outside the interfacing. Cut notches in the corners of the seam allowance.

Iron in the seam allowance. Strips of iron-on double-sided fusible web could possibly be used to attach the seam allowance. Sew with a large seam with a sewing machine to keep the seam allowance temporarily in place. Sew as tightly as possible around the edge if you are not using fusible web strips, ensuring that the seam is able to be removed.

Follow the same procedure with the smaller cut out part and the lining.

YOU WILL NEED
Heavy-weight fusible interfacing with an adhesive side
Fabric for the outside
Fabric for the lining
Strips of iron-on double-sided fusible web
Ribbon
Hook and loop fasteners

Place the lining precisely inside the other piece and fold together as you would for a finished sewing kit. Firstly, fold the right sides together, then fold the left side above. Adjust the folds in the right places, and iron to mark the folds.

Mark where the hook and loop fasteners should be placed in order for them to attach to each other, then fold the pieces out again.

Fold the fabric rights facing and trace a square measuring 16 × 10.5cm (6¼ × 4⅛in). Sew around. Cut out and make a small reverse opening through one of the layers in the middle of the square, then reverse and iron.

Fold and iron the square twice so you will have two pieces for needles, one about 9.5cm (3¾in) and the other about 6.5cm (2½in), with the reverse opening on the underside. Place the folded square in the middle of the piece furthest to the right on the lining and attach on top with a seam, see figure A.

A

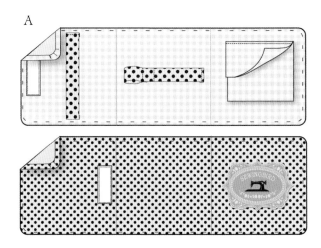

Use a wide ribbon to make loops tailored to fit your sewing equipment, see picture and figure A on pages 30–31. The end of the ribbon in the middle piece of the lining is folded in a way that creates a loose loop to hold scissors. Use your scissors to measure how large the loop should be before you start sewing.

Fold the tip of the ribbon in the opposite end and attach with a seam. You can sew as many seams as you wish to create the loops or space for your equipment. Attach the hook and loop fasteners.

Stitch on a fabric sign to the front side if you wish, see figure A on page 30 and Appliqués on page 8.

Finally, place the pieces wrong sides facing and stitch up with a seam about 3mm (⅛in) from the edge, see figure B.

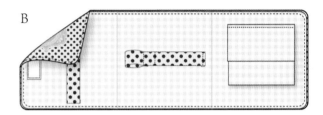

Little Sewing Ideas

PAPER SEWING EQUIPMENT

On page 49 you can find a selection of printable sewing motifs. These can be printed onto good quality sewing paper and glued onto patterned cardboard from Tilda paper pads or similar to create substantial models with a pretty backdrop.

Cut out the models. Fold a piece of fabric and attach it to the needle card using a stapler or similar to create a pretty needle case. The cards make lovely gift tags or can be used for storage for your nicest buttons. Simply sew the buttons to the card.

LAMP SHADE NOTICE BOARD

To create a three-dimensional alternative to the traditional notice board, dress an old lamp shade with 2cm (¾in) wide fabric strips. Attach the ends using a glue gun.

Among the Tilda products you can find paper and décor with a sewing theme, enabling you to make customised cards and decorate gifts for your friends.

See page 46 for gift tag pattern.

Sewing Angel

HOW TO MAKE

DRESS

Follow the instructions for the Garden Party Angels on page 16 up to figure E, where the top of the trouser (pant) suit is attached.

Cut a piece of fabric measuring 66 × 30cm (25¾ × 12in) for the skirt, adding a seam allowance.

Fold the skirt double, right sides facing, making it 30cm (12in) in height and 33cm (13in) in width and stitch up the open side. Reverse the skirt, iron and sew the seam allowance at the bottom up.

Sew along the top edge of the skirt and pucker at the waist. Attach with a few stitches, see figure A.

BELT

Cut a piece of fabric measuring 6 × 30cm (2⅜ × 12in) without a seam allowance. Fold and iron 1cm (⅜in) inwards on each short side and 1cm (⅜in) along each long side, see figure B.

Fold and iron the strip twice to become 1.5cm (⅝in) wide and stitch up the open side, see figure C. Tie the belt tight around the waist. Attach the knot and upper part of the ends with a few stitches to secure and let the two ends hang down, see figure D.

YOU WILL NEED
Fabric for the skin
Fabric for the dress
Fabric for the wings
Fabric for piece of fabric
Mini bobbins
Tilda hair
Wadding (batting)
Thin wooden stick
Adhesive pads
Print of a sewing machine
Glue gun (optional)

Sew and attach the wings as described on page 20. Make the hair and face as described on page 9.

See patterns on pages 42–44.

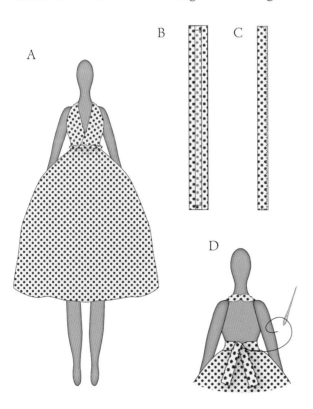

SEWING MACHINE

Print or photocopy the sewing machines from page 48 onto photo cardboard and cut out. Cut a piece of a thin wooden stick to approximately 10cm (4in).

Place the stick to the position that the bobbin is attached to on the sewing machine and attach adhesive pads around it, see figure E. Remove the paper from the adhesive pads and glue the other part of the sewing machine onto these. Thread the bobbin onto the stick, see figure F, using glue to secure if desired.

Cut a piece of fabric measuring 10 × 15cm (4 × 5¾in), adding a seam allowance. Fold the piece right sides facing to measure approximately 10 × 7.5cm (4 × 3in) and stitch up the long side and one of the short sides. Reverse and iron the piece. Fold a few tucks in the piece of fabric and bend it around the sewing machine so it will tack (baste) to itself in the back, see figure G.

The sewing machine can be attached to the angel's hands by carefully pushing the needle and thread between the adhesive pads between the two layers of the sewing machine when you tack (baste). Then attach the upper part of the sewing machine to the dress using tacking (basting) stitches around the bobbin attachment, see figure H. Alternatively, the easiest way is to use a glue gun.

E
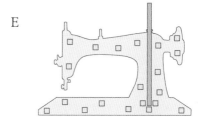

F

G

H

Fabric Boxes

HOW TO MAKE

Trace the pattern four times next to each other on iron-on heavy-weight fusible interfacing. Cut so you will have seam allowance on all sides except the top edge, see figure A.

Cut two pieces of fabric large enough for the whole shape, but add 1.5cm (⅝in) to the fabric strip for the lining and subtract the same on the fabric strip for the outside of the box. This will make a lining border on the outside of the box, see the picture opposite.

Stitch up the two fabric strips and iron a seam allowance in the splice away from each other.

Place the case interfacing piece with the adhesive side against the wrong side of the fabric piece that is sewn together. The interfacing part should be placed against the fabric that is supposed to be on the outside of the box, but 1.5cm (⅝in) in to the lining, see figure B.

Trace the pattern to the lining piece four times, like a mirror image of the interfacing part and against the interfacing parts' edge.

Cut the whole shape, remembering to add a seam allowance to the lining.

Fold one of the boxes with lining so that it lies right sides facing against the next piece, and sew together, see figure C. Continue folding and stitch up the sides to the left. Then place the ends against each other and sew all the way around, leaving one area for reversing the lining, see figure D.

Reverse the box and close the reverse opening with tacking (basting) stitches. Push the lining into the box. Iron the box and press the folds with an iron to achieve a nice shape.

See pattern on page 47.

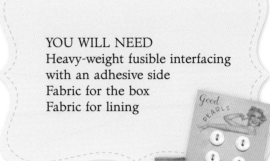

YOU WILL NEED
Heavy-weight fusible interfacing with an adhesive side
Fabric for the box
Fabric for lining

A

B

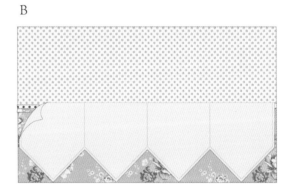

C

D

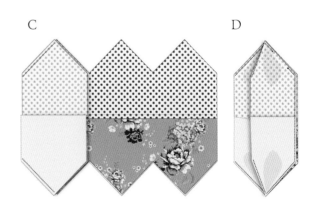

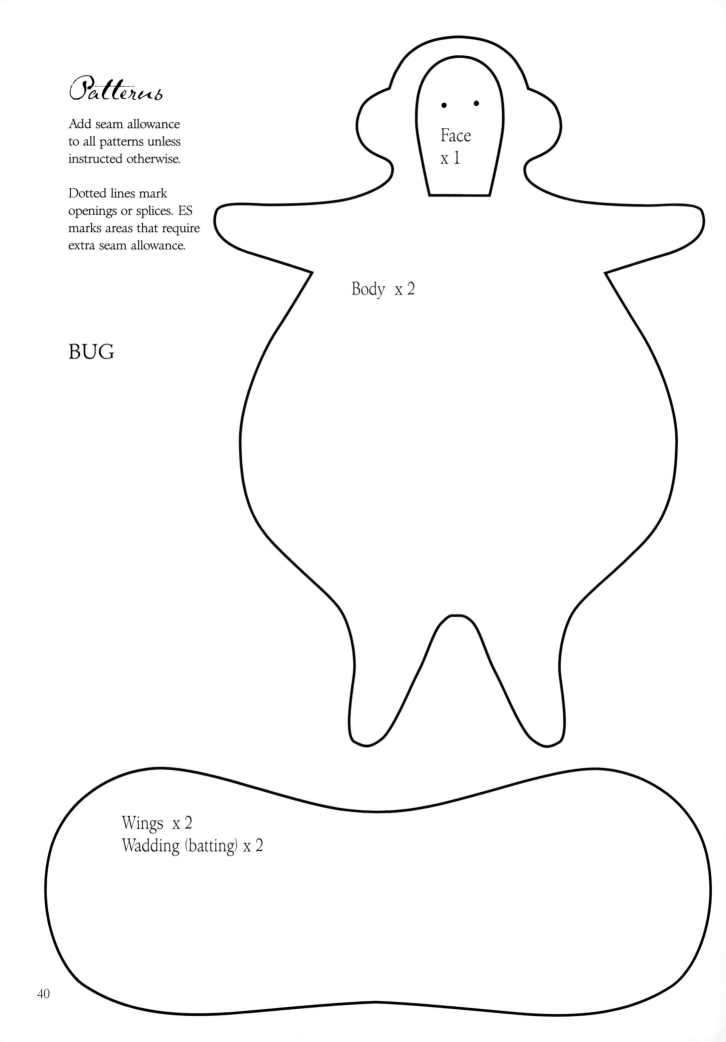

Patterns

Add seam allowance to all patterns unless instructed otherwise.

Dotted lines mark openings or splices. ES marks areas that require extra seam allowance.

BUG

Face x 1

Body x 2

Wings x 2
Wadding (batting) x 2

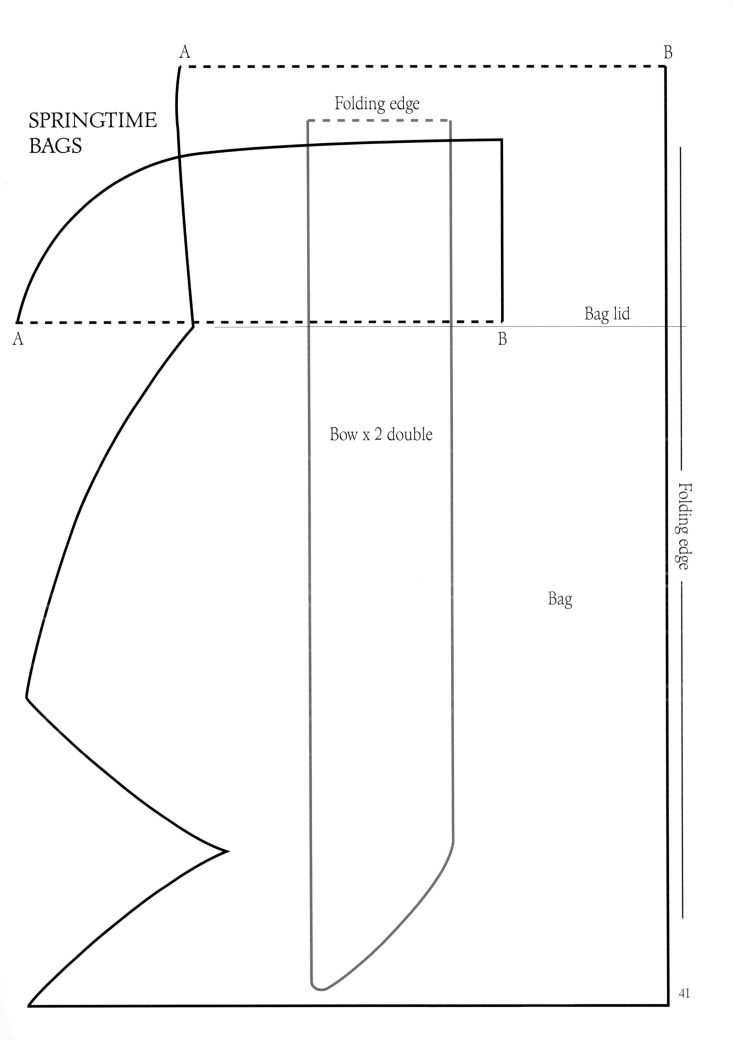

SPRINGTIME
BAGS

A

B

Folding edge

A

B

Bag lid

Bow x 2 double

Folding edge

Bag

41

GARDEN PARTY AND SEWING ANGELS

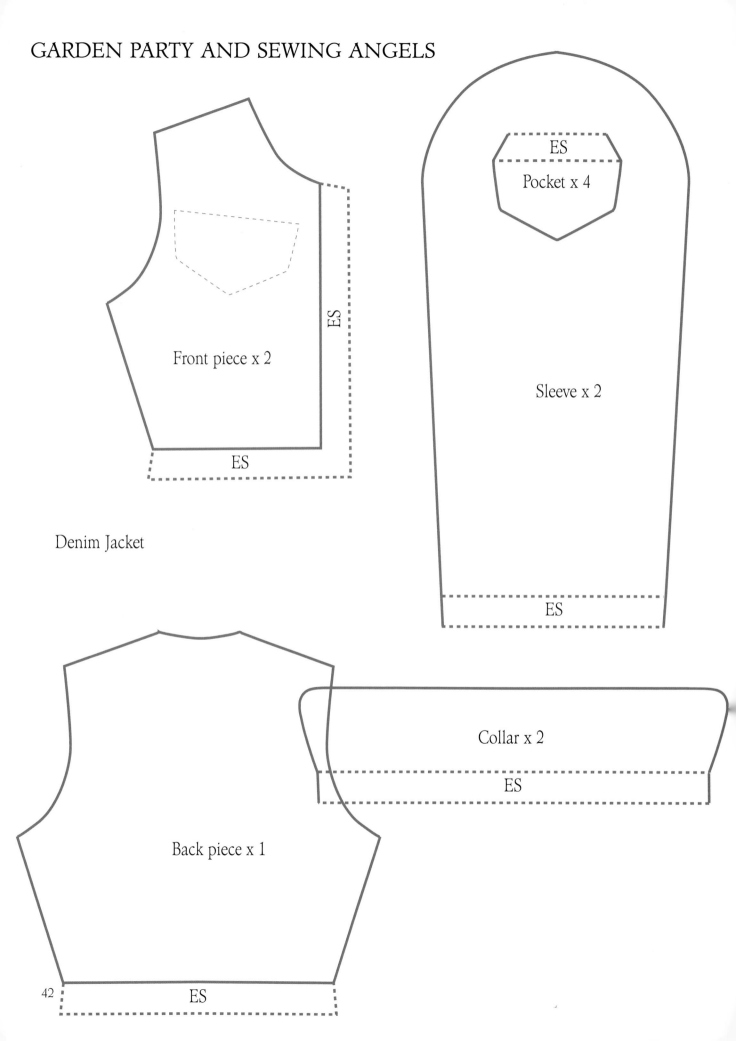

Front piece x 2

ES

ES

ES

Denim Jacket

Pocket x 4

ES

Sleeve x 2

ES

Collar x 2

ES

Back piece x 1

ES

42

GARDEN PARTY AND SEWING ANGELS

A   B

A   B

Body x 2

ES

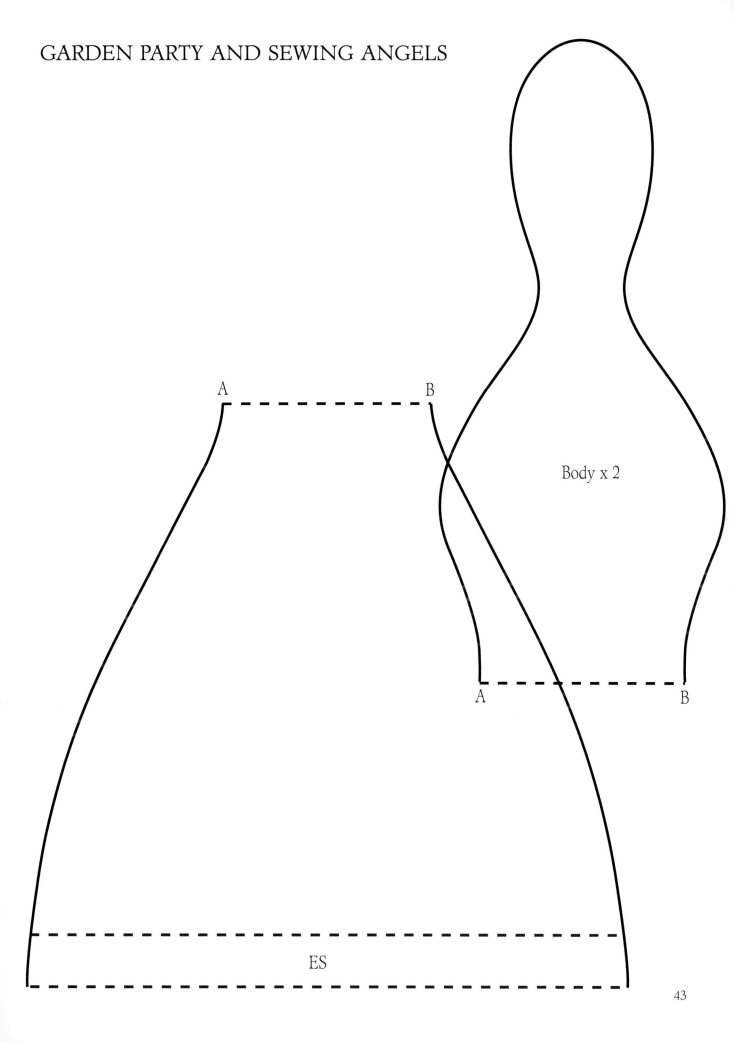

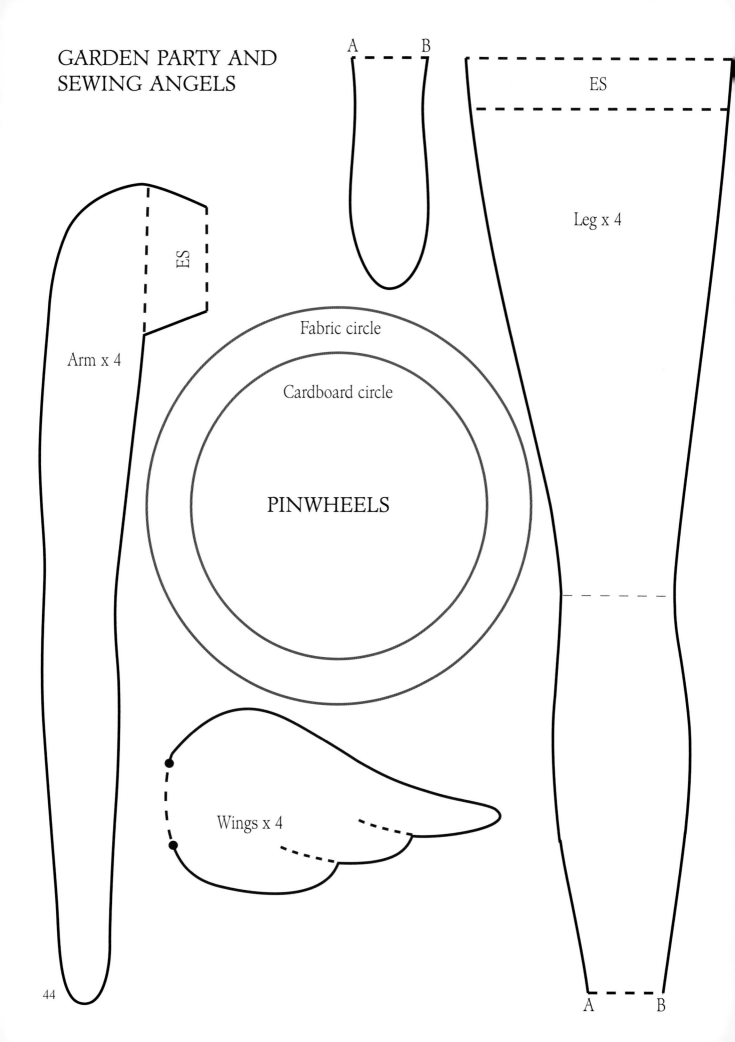

GARDEN PARTY AND
SEWING ANGELS

A   B

ES

Leg x 4

ES

Arm x 4

Fabric circle

Cardboard circle

PINWHEELS

Wings x 4

44

A   B

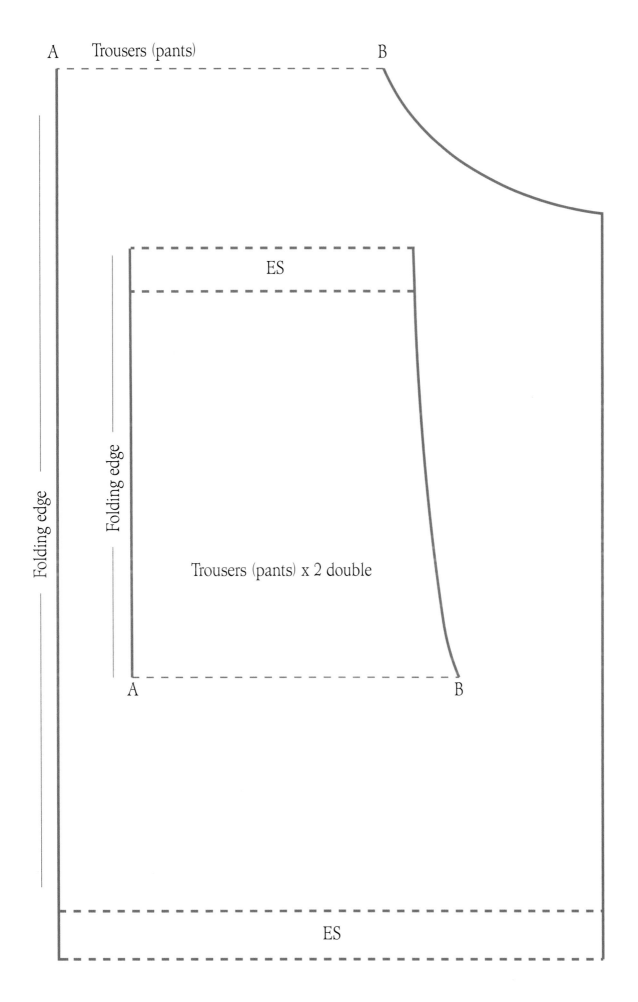

A   Trousers (pants)   B

Folding edge

Folding edge

ES

Trousers (pants) x 2 double

A   B

ES

GIFT BAGS

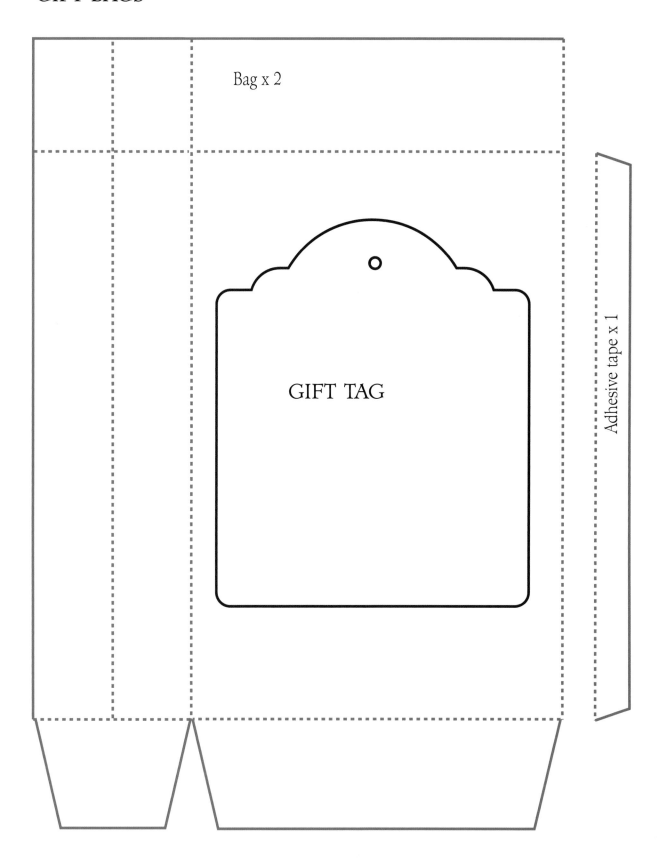

Bag x 2

Adhesive tape x 1

GIFT TAG

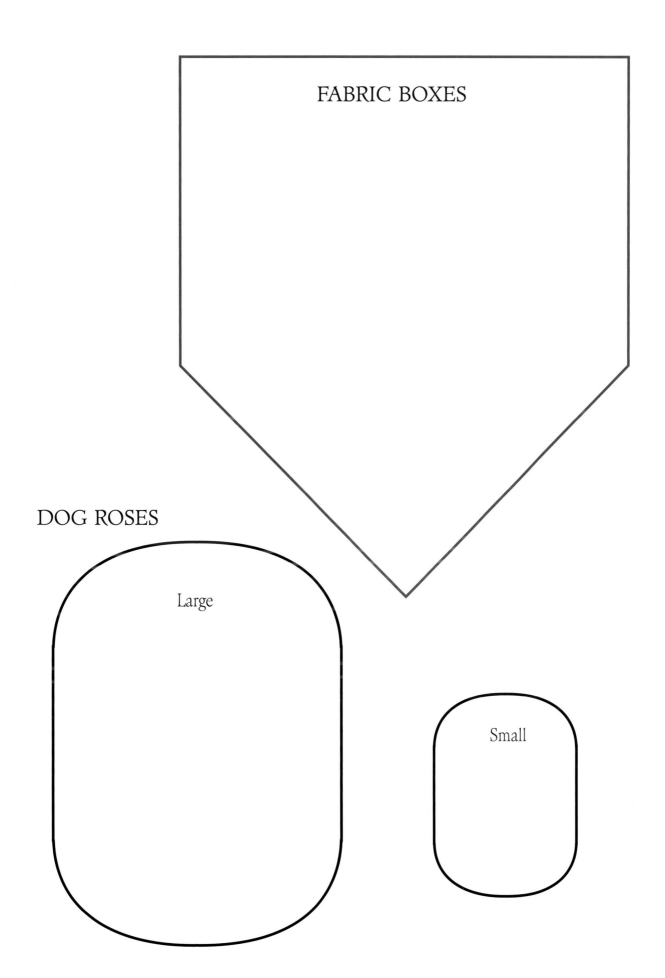

FABRIC BOXES

DOG ROSES

Large

Small

Accessories

These accessories can be copied using a photocopier, or scanned and printed as decorations for the projects in the book (170–200 gsm matt photo paper is recommended).

Sewing Machine for the Sewing Angel

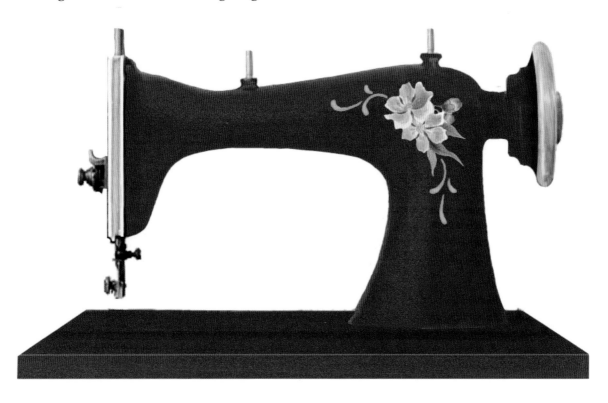

Tilda's
SUMMER
IDEAS

Colourful Summer

Summer is just around the corner and now's the time to start creating lighter and brighter surroundings. At this time of year it feels natural to create with playful colours, capturing the essence of summer.

In this section you will find ideas for garden-inspired angels, a variety of colourful garlands, traditional Swedish Dala horses and some lovely papercraft ideas to help bring some sun and summer into your home!

The projects are made using the Tilda collections Kitchengarden and Flowergarden, using shades of turquoise, green, pink and red. It was a great pleasure designing this Tilda range and I hope you'll find some projects here you'd like to make. But remember, the real value is in the pattern, so feel free to use materials you already have, or combine old and new.

Wishing you a wonderful and creative summer!

Enjoy!

Tone Finnanger

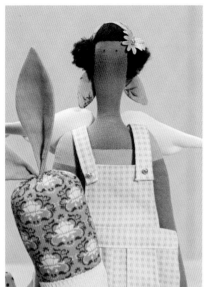

Techniques

HAIR

Make the fringe using the same embroidery yarn as the hair. Embroidery yarn in suitable hair colours is available from the Tilda range. Draw a line using a vanishing marker or a thin pen with pale ink over the forehead, so you have a guide for sewing the fringe. Sew a fringe with small stitches using the embroidery yarn, then sew some longer stitches down over the cheek on each side, see figure A.

FACES

We recommend you add the hair before marking the eyes to ensure they are correctly positioned. Stick two pins into the head to check where the eyes should sit. Remove the pins. Use the eye tool from the Tilda Face Painting set (ref. no. 713400) or make the eyes (where the pinholes are) by dipping a pinhead in some black paint and pressing onto the face. Make rosy cheeks by applying some lipstick or blusher with a dry brush, after the eyes have dried.

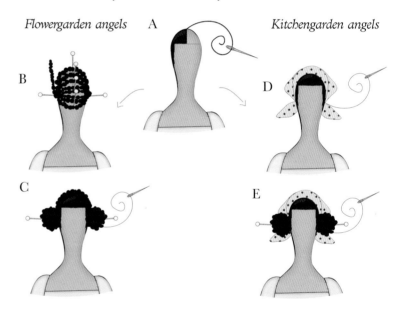

Flowergarden angels   A   *Kitchengarden angels*

B   D

C   E

Flowergarden angels

Stick pins into the forehead and over the centre to the back of the head. Also insert a pin in each side of the head. Wind the hair back and forth between the pins on each side of the head and between the pins in the middle, see figure B. When the head is covered, stitch the hair in place and remove the pins. Then sew a bunch of hair onto each side of the head, see figure C.

Kitchengarden angels

Sew the scarf as described in the instructions. Pin the middle of the scarf to the centre of the head, so the fringe is visible. Fold the middle of the scarf over the back of the head and tie a knot with the sides to hold it in place. Fasten with a few stitches and remove the pin, see figure D. Make a little bunch of hair for each side of the head and sew in place, see figure E.

SEWING

Avoid cutting out the figure beforehand unless absolutely necessary. Fold the fabric double, right sides facing, and transfer the pattern onto it. Mark the openings for reversing.

CUTTING OUT

Cut out the figure with a narrow seam allowance, 3–4mm (⅛in) is ideal. Extra seam allowance is required at the reversing sections, approx 7–8mm (⅜in). Cut notches in the seam allowance where the seam curves sharply.

REVERSING

Use a florist's stick to help with reversing. As a rule, use the blunt end, though the pointed end can be used carefully for small details. To avoid piercing the fabric, just cut off the top millimetre of the tip. Long, thin pieces such as legs can be reversed by pressing the blunt end against the foot, see figure A. Starting at the foot, pull the leg over the stick, see figure B. Continue to pull the leg over the stick until the foot appears at the top. Holding the foot, pull the rest of the leg over until it is completely turned right side out, see figure C. Turn the arms in the same way.

STUFFING

Fold in the extra seam allowance by the openings in the seam, with the exception of the legs for the angels, where the seam allowance is tucked into the body and should not therefore be folded in. Iron the figure.

When stuffing, use your finger to push the wadding (batting) in as far as you can, and use a pen or similar to push into the parts you cannot reach. If the implement is too thin it will just push through the filling.

Push the wadding (batting) loosely into the figure and try to avoid over-stuffing, which will cause lumps to form. Add wadding (batting) to each section until correctly stuffed and continue to add wadding (batting) until you have a perfectly formed figure.

Sew up the openings.

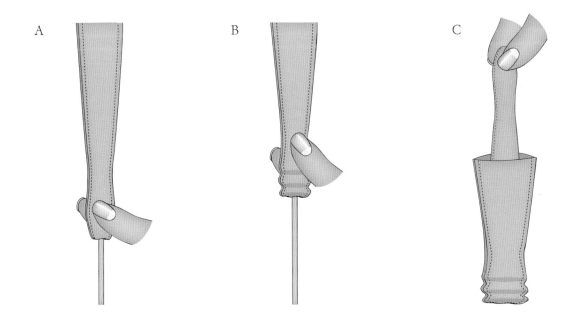

A   B   C

Kitchengarden angels, green cushions and a birdhouse create a cosy summer setting. The birdhouse is part of the Tilda range and can be used as a decoration indoors and a real birdhouse outdoors. We recommend you trim the perch or push it in further to discourage predators.

Seed Sachets

Copy the seed sachet pattern on pages 93–94 onto paper or card. Cut out the sachets and apply glue to the edges. Fold in the glued edges and fold the sachet double to glue it together. Make a hole with a hole punch in the top of the sachet. We recommend that you fold the seeds in paper before placing them in the sachet.

Kitchengarden Angel

YOU WILL NEED
Various fabrics for the skin,
clothes and wings
Wadding (batting)
Tilda hair
Embroidery yarn for the fringe
Craft rubber for sandals
3mm (⅛in) beads or similar
Tilda paper flowers
Lace (optional)

HOW TO MAKE
BODY
Sew together the skin fabric and
the light turquoise fabric so the
join is approximately where shown
in the pattern. Fold the joined
fabrics double, right sides facing.

Do the same with the skin
fabric and the fabric for the arms
and legs. Transfer all patterns, see
figure A.

Cut out all parts and cut
notches in the seam allowance
where it curves sharply.

Reverse the body, arms and
legs as described on page 53.

Iron all sections. The seam
allowance on the body and arms
should be ironed in. Fill the lower
part of the leg with wadding
(batting), until where indicated
by the dashed line in the pattern.
Sew a stitch across the knee
before filling the rest of the leg,
see figure B. Fill the body and
arms. Insert the legs into the body
and sew in place. Sew the arms to
the body, see figure C.

DUNGAREES
Fold fabric for two pockets, upper
section and waistband double.
Transfer the patterns and sew
around, see figure D.

Cut out and reverse. Iron all
the parts. Sew a stitch along the
curved top edge of the pockets
and around the edge of the upper
section, see figure E.

Cut out four trouser (pant)
sections from the patterned green
fabric and four lining sections
from the dotted pink fabric.

Remember that two of the
trouser sections and two of the
lining sections should be reversed.

Sew the lining sections into the
trouser legs so the join between the
trouser and lining is approximately
as shown in the pattern.

See patterns on pages 82–86.

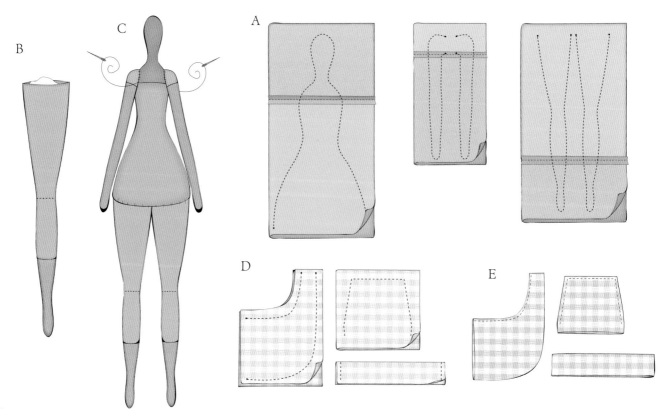

Place the trouser sections together two by two, right sides facing and sew the curved section, see figure F.

Fold out the parts. Sew on the pockets along the lower curved part of the pocket, at the front of the trousers. Sew a zig-zag stitch along the sides, see figure G.

Line up the seam allowance for the waistband and seam allowance for the upper section with the seam allowance for the front of the dungarees. The waistband should be in the middle. Sew a stitch approximately where the

seam allowance ends to attach the three parts, see figure H. Fold up the upper section and fold down and iron the seam allowance at the back of the trouser section.

The waistband should then be folded down over the front of the trousers and cover the top part of the pockets. Sew along the edge to fix the top part of the pockets in place, see figure I.

Place the front of the trousers with the pockets, upper section and waistband, right sides facing, with the trouser backs and sew around, see figure J.

Trim allowances and iron the trousers. Iron in any allowance which is not sewn. Sew around the waist.

Iron in the lining at the bottom of each leg, see figure K. Turn up the bottom, see figure L and fasten with a few stitches inside the trousers.

Cut two strips of patterned green fabric 17 × 3cm (6½ × 1¼in), adding seam allowance. Iron in the allowance along each length and also at one end, then iron each strip double. Sew around the edge of each strip to close the open side.

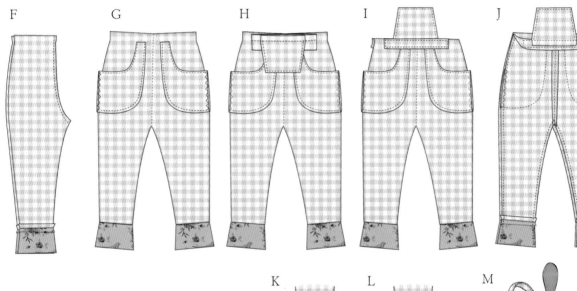

F   G   H   I   J

K   L   M

Put the dungarees on the figure, folding pleats around the waist. Use pins to hold the pleats and then sew the pleats, without sewing to the figure. Remove the pins.

Pin the shoulder straps at the back of the angel and the inside of the trousers. Cross them over at the back. Ensure the trousers are hanging at the correct length before fastening the straps with a bead at the upper section and then sewing at the back, see figure M.

SCARF
Fold the fabric for the scarf with right sides facing, transfer the pattern and sew round, see figure N on page 60. Cut out, reverse and iron.

Add the hair, fasten the scarf and create the face as described on page 52. Make the sandals as described on page 70.

59

WINGS

Fold the fabric for the wings double and transfer the pattern. Sew around the wings, see figure O.

Reverse and iron. Sew the seams as shown in the pattern, see figure P. Fill the wings with wadding (batting) using the wooden stick and close the opening. Sew the wings onto the figure.

CLOTH

Fold the fabric for the cloth with right sides facing and sew three sides.

Cut out and reverse. Iron the cloth. Sew a piece of lace along the bottom edge, see figure Q. Sew the top of the cloth inside the pocket.

Sew a small flower into the angel's hair with a small bead. Sew a piece of lace around each leg. Put the hands inside the pockets, see figure R.

N

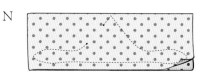

O

P

Q

R

60

Radishes

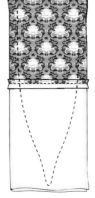

YOU WILL NEED
Fabric for radishes
Fabric for leaves
Wadding (batting)
Lace, if using

HOW TO MAKE
Sew together a strip of pink/red fabric and a strip of white fabric so the border between the two is approximately where shown in the pattern.

Fold the sewn section double, right sides facing and transfer the radish pattern.

Sew around, see figure A. Fold fabric for leaves double, right sides facing, transfer patterns for two leaves and sew around.

Cut out, reverse and iron the radish and leaves. Iron in the seam allowance at the radish's opening.

Sew around the opening with embroidery yarn. Stuff the radish and insert the leaves before sewing up the opening, see figure B. Sew a few stitches to fasten the leaves and pull the yarn tight.

If using, sew some lace around the radish.

See patterns on page 88.

61

Summer Garlands

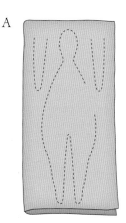

YOU WILL NEED
Fabric for the skin
Tilda hair
Embroidery yarn for hair
Fabric for dresses
Flower buttons
Wadding (batting)
Radishes, see page 61
Ribbon for hanging

Fill the body and arms and
sew up the opening in the body.
Sew the arms onto each side of the
figure, see figure B.

See patterns on page 89.

HOW TO MAKE
BODY
Fold the skin fabric double, transfer
the pattern and sew round the
body and arms, see figure A.

You will need at least two
figures to make the garland. Cut
out, fold inside out and iron the
parts. Iron in the seam allowance at
the opening on the arms.

B

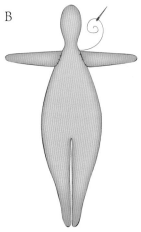

DRESS

Cut two pieces of fabric for the dress 15.5 × 17cm (6¼ × 6½in), adding plenty of seam allowance at each end. Measure approx 6cm (2½in) below one end at each side of each dress section and fold in the corners so the edge folds over the top. Iron the top edge, insert a piece of embroidery yarn approx 40cm (16in) in length, and sew up, see figure C.

Do the same with the other dress fabric and insert the same length of yarn. Position the dress with right sides facing and sew up the side. Iron and sew up the seam allowance at the base of the dress, see figure D. Reverse the dress, put onto the figure and tie the ends of the embroidery yarn at one end so the dress is pulled tight around the neck, see figure E.

Make three radishes from page 61, or three hearts between the figures. Make the hearts by folding the fabric, right sides facing, transferring the pattern and sewing around. Cut out, reverse, iron and fill. Sew up the opening, then sew the figures together and tie a ribbon at each end to hang from.

C   D   E

Make this beautiful summer setting in your kitchen in the shades of turquoise, red and pink. The Flowergarden Angel can be found on page 70.

FLAG GARLANDS

Using embroidered flower appliqués from the Tilda range and pom-pom ribbon, we've given this flag garland a modern twist. Fold the fabric for the flag, right sides facing, then transfer the flag pattern and sew up the sides. Cut out, reverse and iron. Sew a zig-zag stitch along the open end to hold it together.

Cut a strip of fabric as long as you want the garland to be, and 4.5cm (1¾in) wide. Iron in approx 7mm (⅜in) on each side of the strip and iron it double to make it approx 1.5cm (⅝in) wide. Insert the flag edges with zig-zag stitching in between the two layers of the strip and pin in place. Sew along the open side of the strip to fasten the flags in place. Sew the pom-pom ribbon along the bottom edge of the strip and sew the flower appliqué onto some of the flags.

See patterns on page 87.

LANTERNS

We recommend you use a glass which is relatively straight. Measure the circumference around the top and bottom of the glass, plus its height, and transfer the measurements onto card. Cut out and check that the pattern fits the glass. Transfer the pattern onto fabric and add seam allowance when cutting out.

Iron in the seam allowance at the top and bottom with Vlisofix or stitch to fasten. Fold the fabric, right sides facing, and sew up the open side. Pull the fabric over the glass from the narrowest end up and decorate by sewing or gluing on ribbon, beads and appliqué.

Bags

YOU WILL NEED
Fabric for bag, handle and lining
Extra stiff bag Vlisofix
Fabric and ribbon for decoration (optional)

HOW TO MAKE
The striped decoration on the bag is done in the same way as on the hearts, see page 76. Decorate the front bag section before sewing the bag together. The bag and lining pattern is marked double fold and should be double. The bag pattern is wider than the lining pattern, as the bag fabric will be hemmed along the edge.

Cut out two bag sections and two lining sections in your chosen fabrics. Cut out two pieces of stiff Vlisofix measuring 19.5 × 7.5cm (7¾ × 3in) with seam allowance only along the ends, and cut out

pieces of fabric measuring 19.5 × 15cm (7¾ × 6in) with seam allowance all the way round. Place the glue side of the bag, Vlisofix against one half of the fabric and iron on. Iron the seam allowance along one edge around the Vlisofix, see figure A. Take one bag section with Vlisofix and the lining and sew up, see figure B.

Sew a large stitch along the top edge of the bag section to enable you to pull the string tight. Gather the fabric so that the bag is the same width as the lining and edge.

Place the edge where the fabric is ironed in over the gathered edge of the bag section. Fasten with pins and sew, see figure C.

Place the two bag sections with right sides facing and sew around, leaving the opening in the lining.

HANDLE
Cut a piece of bag Vlisofix 30 × 2cm (12 × ¾in) without seam allowance, and a piece of fabric 30 × 4cm (12 × 1½in), with plenty of seam allowance. Place the Vlisofix strip against one half of the fabric strip. Fold in the seam allowance along each side and fold the fabric strip double around the Vlisofix, see figure D. Sew a stitch along the open edge to fasten the layers.

Trim allowances, reverse and iron the bag. Push the lining down inside the bag.

Fasten the end of the handle onto each side inside the bag with pins. Sew a stitch around the top edge of the bag to fasten the handles and hold the lining in place, see figure D.

See patterns on page 91.

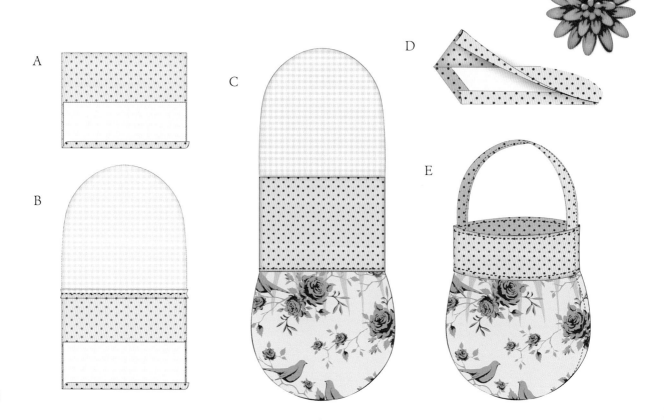

A

B

C

D

E

68

Flowergarden Angel

See patterns on pages 82–83 and page 88.

YOU WILL NEED
Different fabrics for the skin, clothes and wings
Tilda hair
Embroidery yarn for hair
Craft rubber for sandals
3mm (⅛in) beads or similar
Tilda paper flowers

HOW TO MAKE
Sew the body and wings in the same way as for the Kitchengarden Angel on page 56 and do the hair and face as described on page 52.

DRESS
Cut a piece of floral fabric 26 × 52cm (10½ × 20¾in), adding plenty of seam allowance. Fold the fabric double to make it 26 × 26cm (10½ × 10½in) and sew the opposite open side, see figure A.

A

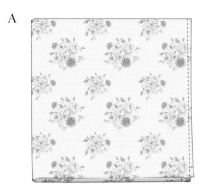

B

Reverse the dress and iron in the seam at the top and bottom. Sew up the seam allowance at the bottom.

Pin the dress around the midriff with small pleats. The dress should sit quite high up, see picture of the angel. Sew the dress around the body.

Fold the fabric for the belt double and transfer the pattern. Sew around the belt, remembering to leave a gap to turn it inside out, see figure B.

Cut out, reverse and iron the belt. Tie the belt around the angel's chest, with the knot to one side. Fasten with a few stitches so the ends sit nicely, see figure C.

Sew on the wings and sew on a paper flower and beads by the belt knot and in the hair, see figure D.

SANDALS
Copy the pattern for two sandals onto the craft rubber and cut out. Attach the craft rubber sandals with a few stitches under the foot. Attach a small flower with a bead in the middle of each sandal, see figure E.

C

D

E

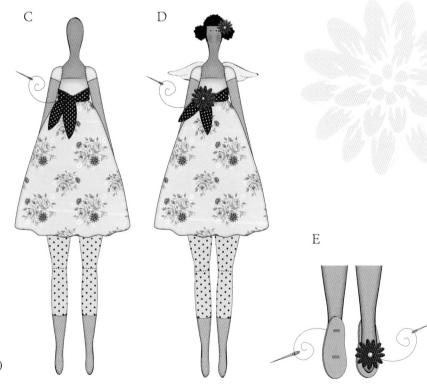

Dala Horses

YOU WILL NEED
Fabric for the body and mane
Vlisofix
Wadding (batting)
Fabric or ribbon for decoration
Embroidery yarn
Beads for decoration

HOW TO MAKE
Embroidered details can be added before the horse is sewn together, but as the fabric stretches slightly, it is easier to do it at the end.

Cut two pieces of fabric large enough for the head and two pieces large enough for the body, using contrasting fabrics. Sew the head fabric and body fabric together so the border is approximately where shown in the pattern. Place the two body parts with right sides facing and sew around, see figure A.

Cut out, reverse, iron and stuff the horse. Iron Vlisofix against the wrong side of a piece of fabric for the mane. Transfer the pattern from the pattern and cut out, without seam allowance. Iron the mane onto the horse.

Transfer the embroidery pattern as closely as possible with a vanishing marker or thin pen on the mane and head. Embroider with embroidery yarn in your chosen colour, as shown in the picture. Hide the knots at the seam between the head and body details where the ribbon will sit.

Cut strips of fabric 2cm (¾in) wide plus seam allowance to use as ribbon. Iron in the seam allowance and sew the ribbon around the belly and neck of the horse. If you wish, sew a string of beads around the ribbon around the neck.

Trim the stick on a figure stand to the required length, sharpen the tip with a pencil sharpener and twist into the horse to enable it to stand stably.

See patterns on page 92.

A

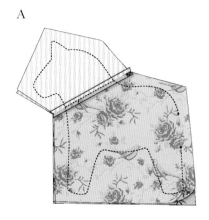

Summer Cushions

YOU WILL NEED
Various complementary fabrics
Volume Vlisofix (optional)
Ribbon or flower appliqué
(optional)

HOW TO MAKE
If you don't have inner cushions suitable for the shape you want to sew, iron a layer of volume Vlisofix against the wrong side of the cushion fabric for an even result. The cushion can then be filled with wadding (batting). A quick solution for the impatient souls among us...

Square cushions do not need more detailed instructions, but in the picture you can see how you can use different fabrics together to make a range of matching cushions. Accompany with a few candle lanterns using the same fabric range and you'll soon have a brand new sitting room!

SIMPLE ROLL CUSHION
Cut out a centre fabric measuring approximately 44 × 44cm (17½ × 17½in), and two side fabrics measuring 44 × 10cm (17½ × 4in). Add seam allowance. Iron volume Vlisofix against the centre fabric to achieve a better shape. Sew the side fabrics to the centre fabric.

Fold in approx 5cm (2½in) of the seam allowance on the outside of each end of the side pieces.

Iron in the seam allowance along the length and then fold a 2cm (¾in) edge to make a tunnel for the cord. Sew the edge in place and thread the cord through, see figure A.

Sew on a ribbon, see figure B, before folding the cushion with right sides facing and sew up the open side. Reverse and iron the cushion. Draw the cords tight and tie. Decorate the cushion with a flower appliqué, if using.

A

B

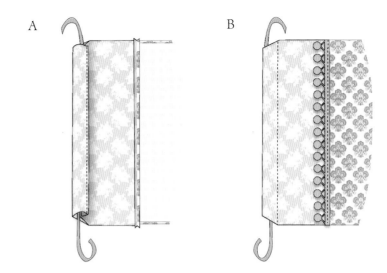

Hearts

YOU WILL NEED
Fabric for the hearts
Various fabrics and ribbons
for decoration
Wadding (batting)
Ribbon for hanging

HOW TO MAKE
Sewing strips of fabric and ribbon
into shapes might not seem too
exciting, but believe me, it's really
great fun! Perhaps because you
can get super results very quickly

and you can play with so many
different colours and patterns. Try
using other patterns, as shown on
page 69.

Cut two pieces of fabric large
enough for the heart.

Find some suitable ribbons
and cut strips of leftover fabric.
Iron in the edges of the fabric
strips, see figure A. Place the
strip on the background and pin
in place, see figure B. Sew along
both sides of the ribbons and
fabric strips to fasten.

Iron the decorated fabric piece
thoroughly and place it against
the back piece, right sides facing.

Transfer the heart pattern and
sew around, see figure C.

Cut out, reverse and fill the
heart. Sew up the opening and
sew on a ribbon for hanging.

See patterns on page 90.

A

B

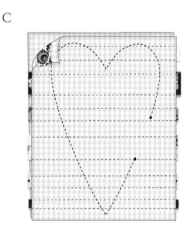

C

Papercraft Ideas

NOTEBOOKS

Cut approximately ten sheets of copier paper in half so that you have twenty sheets in A5 size.

Cut two pieces of decorative card in the same size. Place a pile of sheets between the two pieces of card on either side. Staple together the pile along one side. Staple from both sides if the staples do not go all the way through.

Hammer the stapled side to avoid any rogue staples sticking out. Cut a strip of card which is the same length as the book and approximately 3–4cm (1¼–1½in) wide. Glue the strip around the spine with double-sided tape to hide the staples.

BOOKMARKS

The bookmarks are made from the Tilda decoupage papers and laminated with self-laminating sheets.

Make the tassel by wrapping a bunch of embroidery yarn around your hand. Tie a piece of yarn through the bunch and another around the bunch, before cutting the ends to make tassels.

PRESENTS AND CARDS

Beautiful cards and gifts are always fun to give away. The notebooks on page 78 make gorgeous gifts and here you can see a few versions using green card.

The motifs on the cards are attached with adhesive foam pads for a 3D effect. The edges on the motifs and the cards have been darkened with a brown ink pad.

Patterns

Add seam allowance to all parts of the patterns.

The dashed line marks openings and borders between two different fabrics or where two pattern parts should be sewn together.

ES stands for extra seam allowance and marks openings where this is required.

"Double fold" means that the fabric should be folded double at this line.

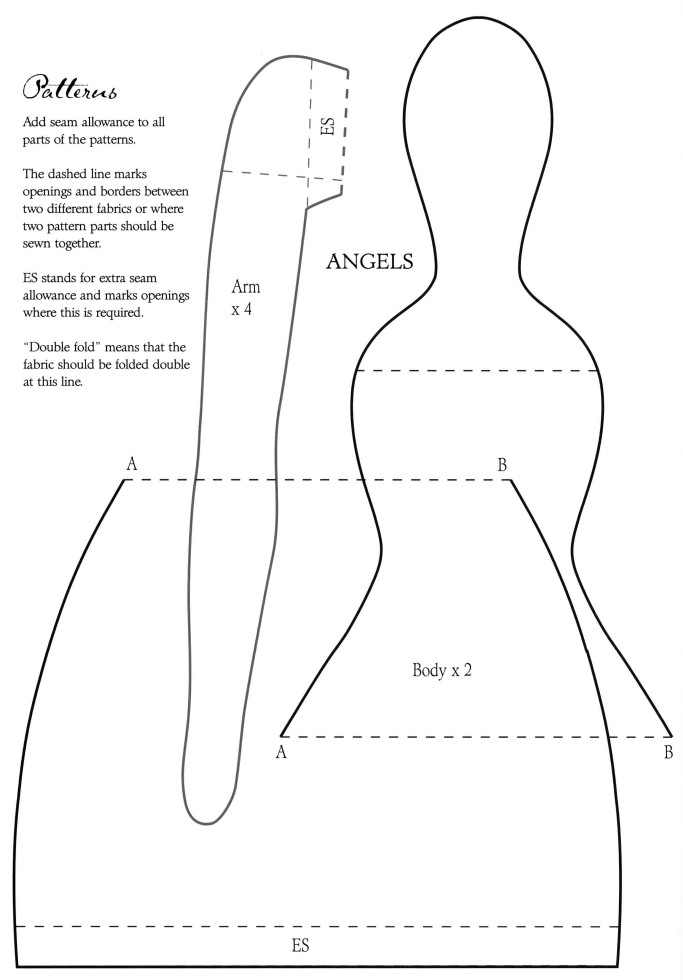

ES

ANGELS

Arm x 4

A

B

Body x 2

A

B

ES

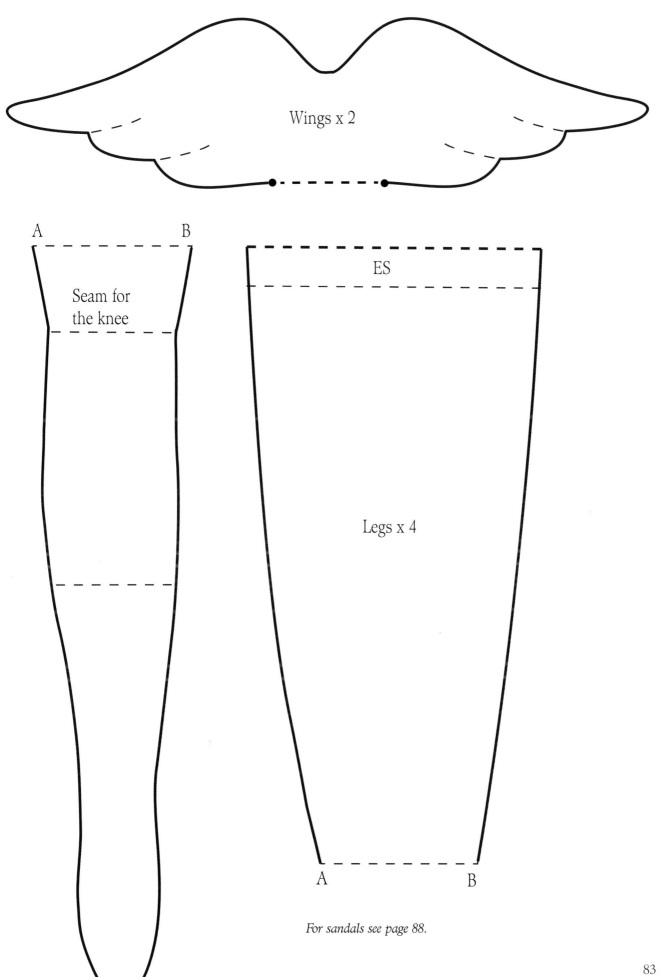

Wings x 2

A   B

Seam for
the knee

ES

Legs x 4

A   B

For sandals see page 88.

KITCHENGARDEN ANGEL ACCESSORIES

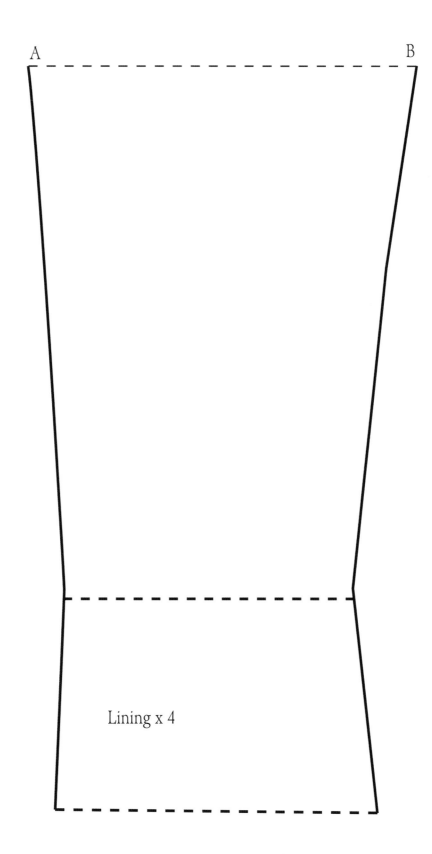

Lining x 4

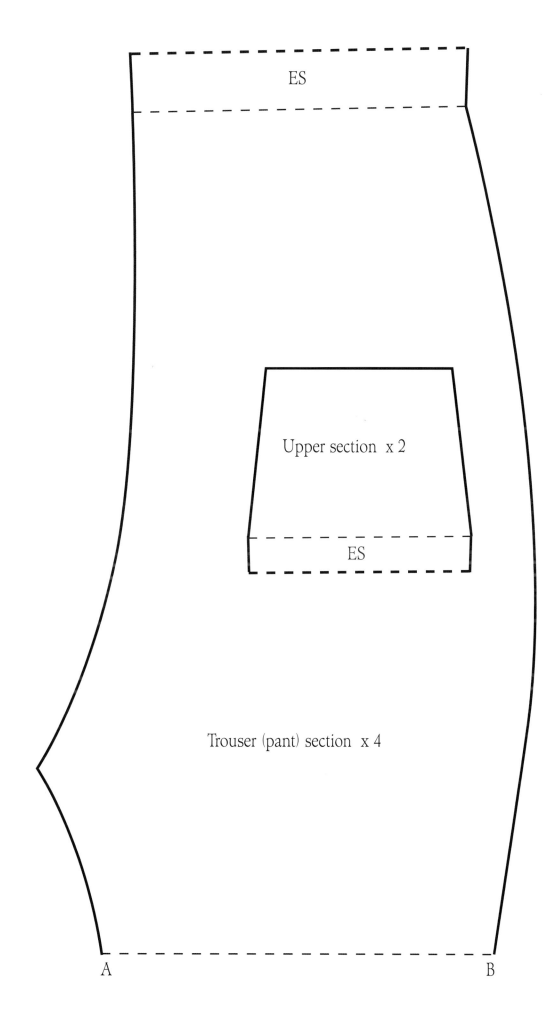

ES

Upper section x 2

ES

Trouser (pant) section x 4

A   B

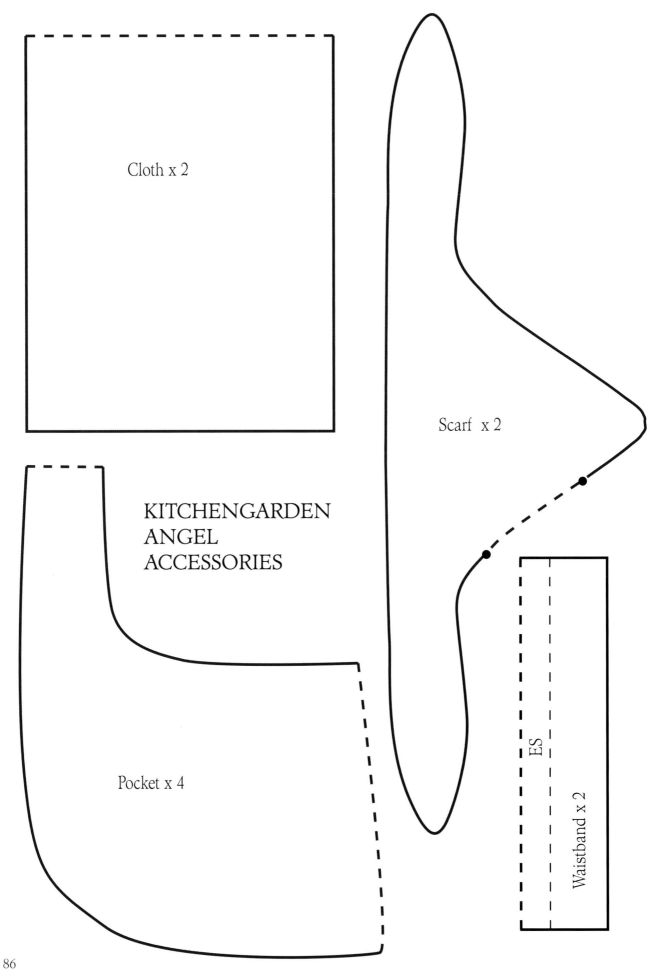

Cloth x 2

Scarf x 2

KITCHENGARDEN
ANGEL
ACCESSORIES

Pocket x 4

ES

Waistband x 2

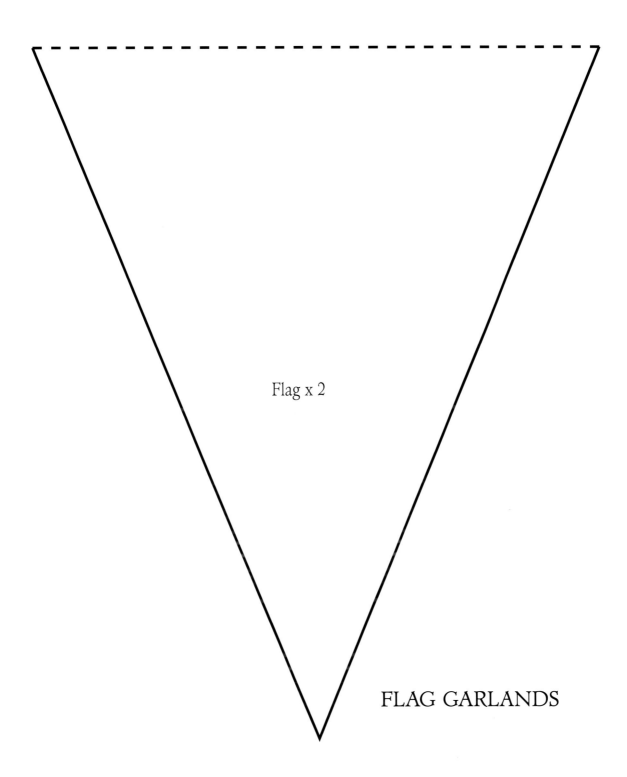

Flag x 2

FLAG GARLANDS

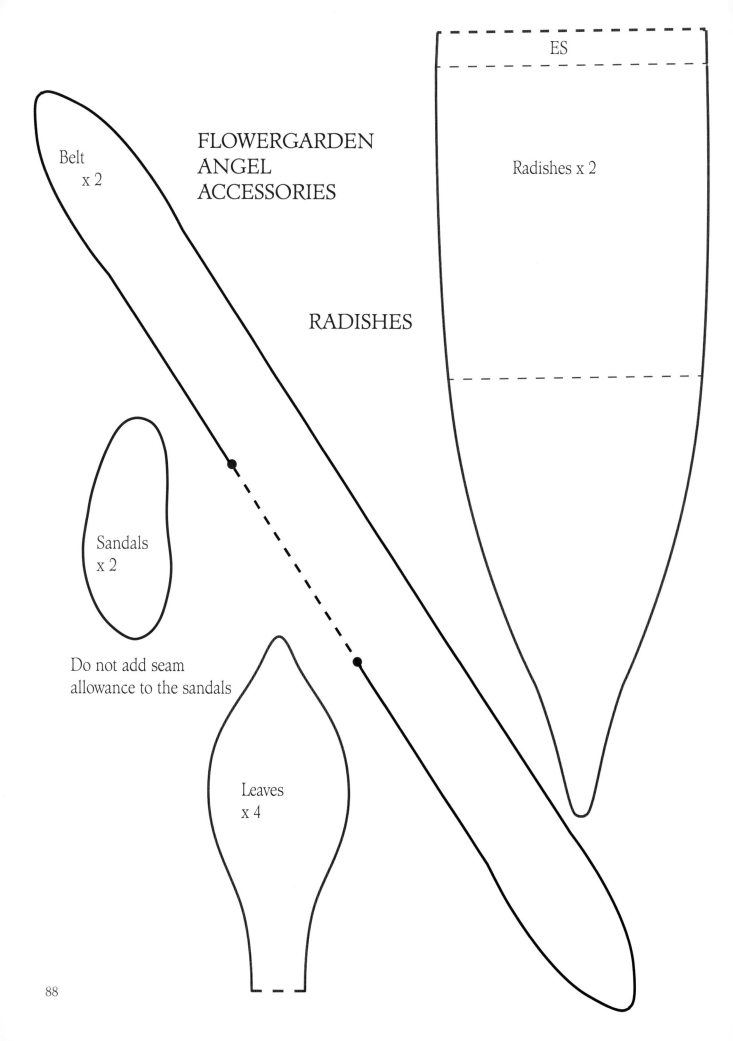

Belt
x 2

FLOWERGARDEN
ANGEL
ACCESSORIES

RADISHES

ES

Radishes x 2

Sandals
x 2

Do not add seam
allowance to the sandals

Leaves
x 4

SUMMER GARLANDS

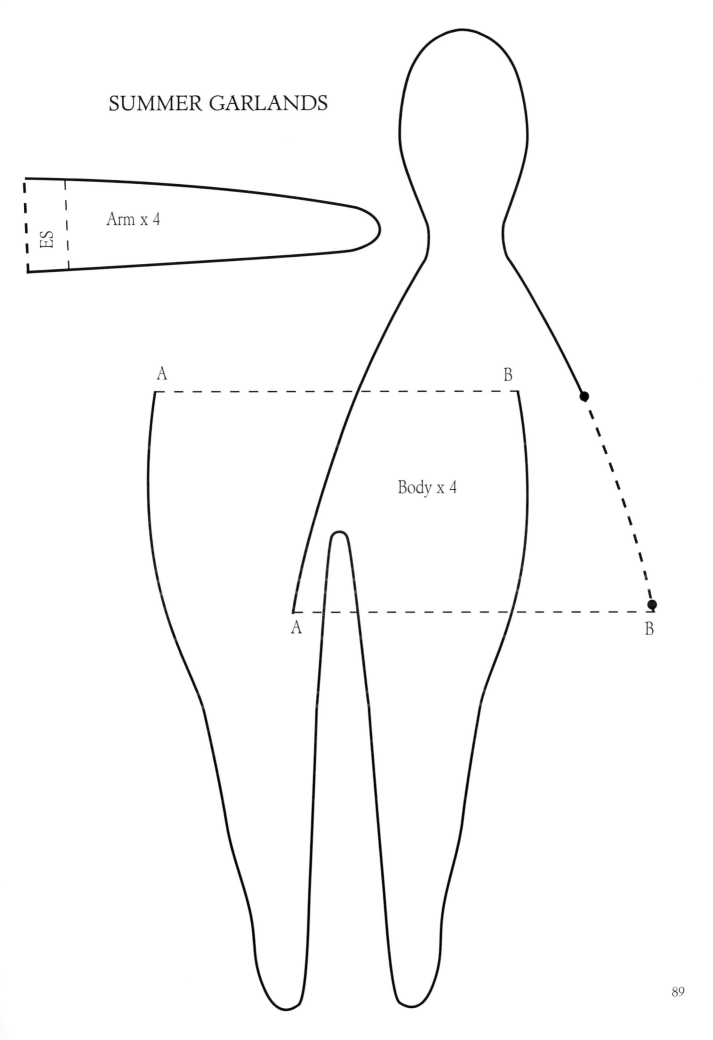

Arm x 4

ES

A   B

Body x 4

A   B

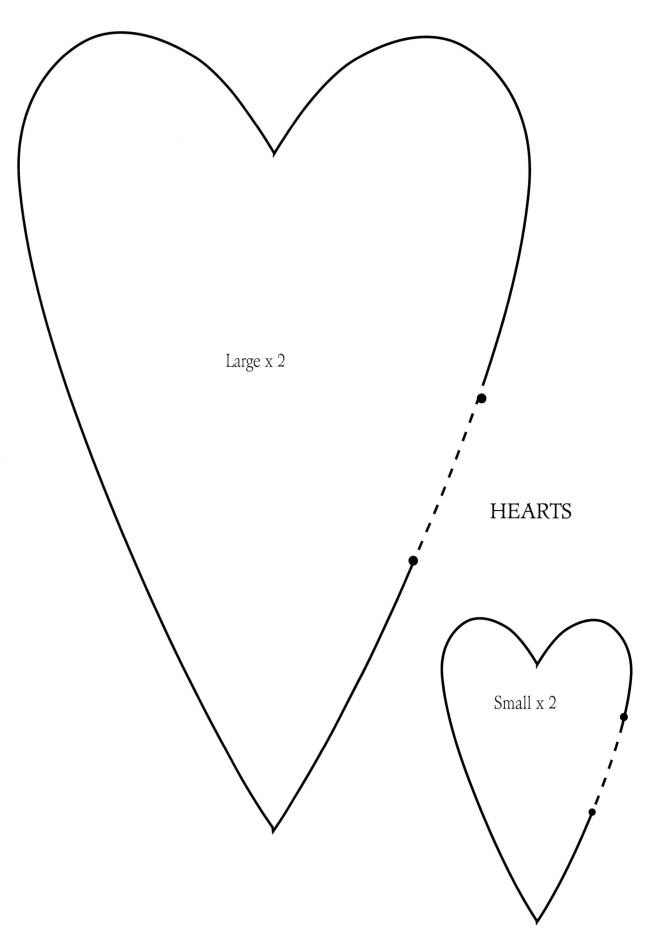

Large x 2

HEARTS

Small x 2

BAG

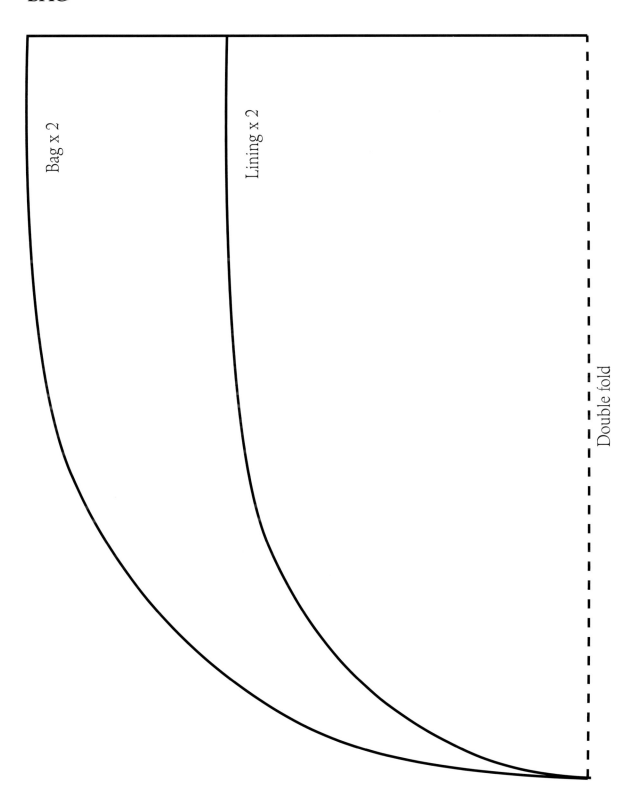

Bag x 2

Lining x 2

Double fold

DALA HORSE

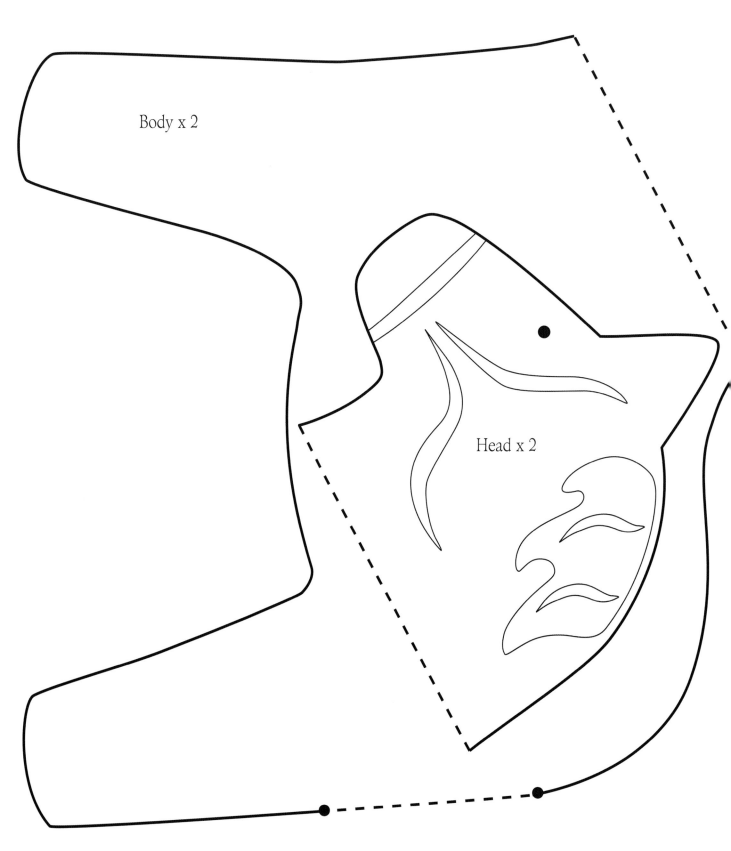

Body x 2

Head x 2

Accessories

These accessories can be copied using a photocopier, or scanned and printed as decorations for the projects in the book (170–200 gsm matt photo paper is recommended).

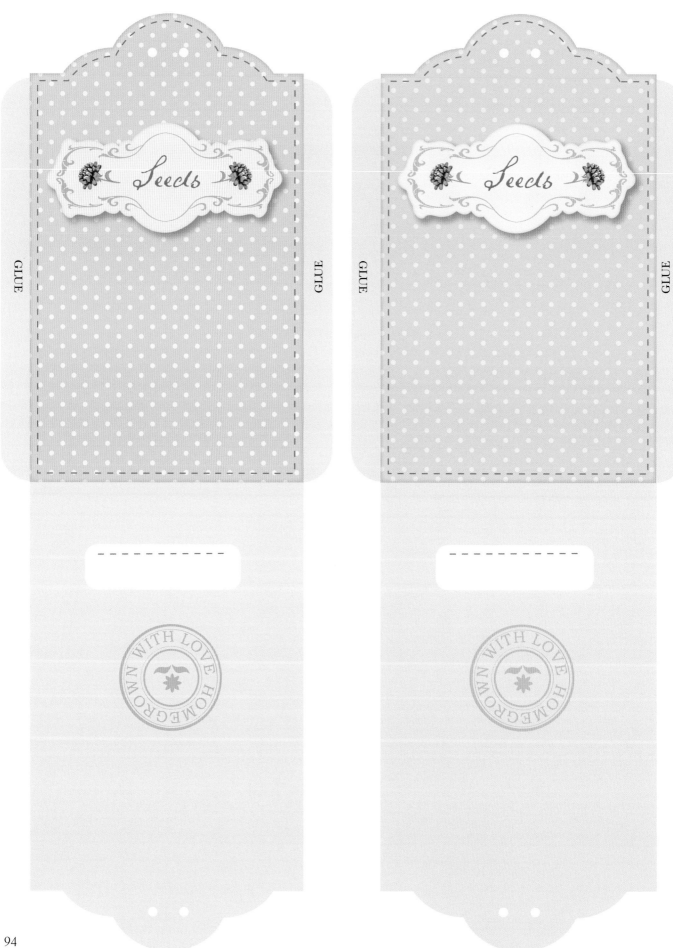

GLUE

GLUE

GLUE

GLUE

94

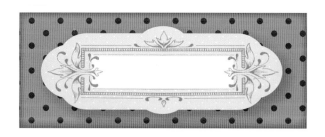

Tilda's
WINTER
IDEAS

Winter Wishes

Christmas is not the same without a nice Christmas workshop with family and friends. From experience I know it's wise to plan ahead and send invitations to the workshop before the most intense Christmas shopping begins. That way everybody can relax and enjoy.

In this section you will find ideas for decorations and gifts – large and small sewing projects like different Santas, Christmas stockings and angels that you can make with your friends. Other simple projects like homemade ribbons, soaps and chocolate gifts are suitable for a more impromptu workshop.

If you want to combine the workshop with food and wine, it might be a good idea to make easy projects that won't require too much effort, like cards and paper decorations.

In this section I chose to use paper wings on some of the figures as they are very small and would be difficult to sew. You will find illustrations for the wings at the end of the section. Instead of paper wings, you could also use little twigs, raffia or buy ready-made wings at a craft store.

Have a fun Christmas!

Tone Finnanger

Stuffed Figures

SEWING

Avoid cutting out parts for the stuffed figures before you start sewing. Instead, fold the fabric right sides together and draw the figure or the parts for the body using the pattern. Sew along the drawn line.

CUTTING OUT

Cut out the figure, including about 3–4mm (¹⁄₈in) seam allowance and 8–10mm (³⁄₈in) allowance across the openings. Cut notches next to the seam around inside curves, see figure A.

It can be a good idea to sew a double seam if it is likely to be under extra pressure when you stuff the shape, like along the neck for the Santas and angels.

REVERSING

Use a wooden stick or something similar to help you turn the figures right sides out. Turn out the arms and legs by pushing the blunt end of the wooden stick towards the tip of the limb, see figure B.

Start closest to the foot/hand and pull the leg/arm down the wooden stick, see figure C.

Hold the foot/hand and pull at the same time as you hold at the bottom so the arm/leg is turned inside out, see figure D. Use the wooden stick to help stuff the parts.

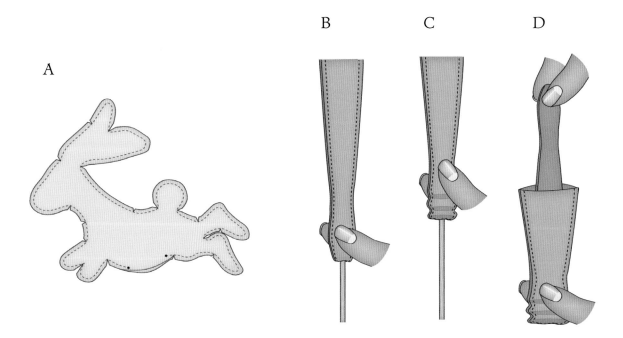

A B C D

Angel Hair

Start by sewing a fringe across the face with embroidery thread in the same colour as the hair, see figure A. Attach pins on the forehead and down the middle of the back of the head. Also attach a pin on each side of the head. Twist hair back and forth between the pins on each side and divide it between the pins in the middle, see figure B. Once the head is covered, stitch the hair down and remove the pins. Make two bundles of hair and attach one to each side of the head, see figure C.

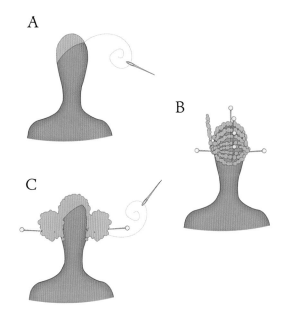

Faces

Make faces by using pins to find out where the eyes should be. Pull out the pins. Dip the eye tool from the Tilda Face Painting set or the head of a small pin in black paint and stamp on the eyes over the pinholes.
Apply Tilda rouge, lipstick or similar with a dry brush to make rosy cheeks.

Paper Wings

On page 141 you will find patterned wings for the Mini Angel and Winter Bunny. You can scan and print out the wings, or make a copy. For one set of wings you need two copies, four wings all together.
Cut out the four wings and glue them wrong sides together so you have the pattern on both sides of each wing. Attach the wings to the figure using adhesive, a glue gun or with a button.

Holiday Spirit

I want to have a Christmas atmosphere in my living room, but I try to avoid the traditional red Christmas decorations. In this chapter I have used warm soft turquoise colours together with glitter and angel motifs as Christmas decorations.

You will find ideas like a gingerbread house made of cardboard and fabric that you can enjoy year after year. Miniature angels and purses will make cute presents for your friends. Small décor projects, gift ideas like homemade ribbons and decorations will create a cosy Christmas atmosphere in your home.

Warm winter wishes

Winter Bunny

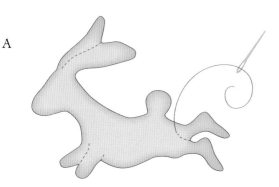

HOW TO MAKE

Read more about stuffed figures on page 98.
Fold a piece of fabric large enough for two rabbit shapes right sides together. Trace the rabbit from the pattern and remember to mark the opening. Sew around the rabbit and cut out.

Use a wooden stick or similar and turn the rabbit right sides out. Iron the rabbit and use the wooden stick to help you stuff it. When you are done stuffing it, use an iron to press the rabbit flat.

YOU WILL NEED
Fabric
Paper wings (see page 99)
Toy stuffing
String for a hanger
Ribbons or paper rose for decorations

See pattern on page 130.

A

Stitch through the rabbit to make the dotted lines shown on the pattern, see figure A.

Make wings as described on page 99. Attach a length of string to the body as a hanger so the rabbit will hang nicely.

A paper rose is used to decorate this rabbit.

Mini Angel

HOW TO MAKE

Fold the skin fabric right sides together and trace the body, arms and legs from the pattern. Cut out and sew around the seam. Turn out and iron the parts. Iron under the seam allowance at the openings for legs and arms. Stuff the parts.

Place the legs inside the body and stitch. Stitch the arms to the body, see figure A. Cut a strip of fabric approximately 11 × 4cm (4¼ × 1½in). Fold the strip in half lengthwise and attach it around the angel's body with a couple of stitches at the back, see figure B. Cut a piece of fabric for the skirt measuring 28 × 10cm (11 × 4in), adding a seam allowance. Fold the piece right sides together widthwise and sew up the back seam. Iron under the seam allowances along the top and bottom edges of the skirt and stitch the bottom hem. Tack (baste) around the top of the skirt and gather it around the waist of the angel. Stitch it in place.

YOU WILL NEED
Fabric for the skin
Fabric for the dress
Paper wings (see page 141)
Tilda hair or similar
Embroidery thread in the same colour as the hair
Toy stuffing
String for a hanger

See patterns on page 129.

Make the hair, face and paper wings as described on page 99. Attach a length of string as a hanger.

The angels can be decorated with glitter glue and Tilda patterned papers.

A

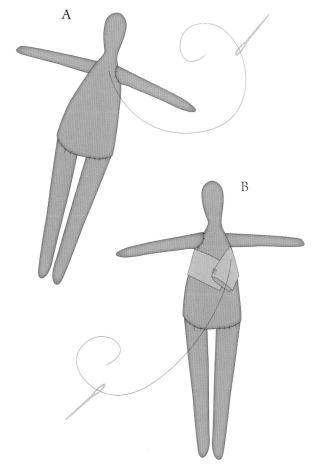

B

104

Gift Ideas

HOMEMADE RIBBONS

Make homemade ribbons by cutting strips of fabric the same width and sew them together for the desired length. Use a rotary cutter to make this easier. Finish the ribbons by sewing a zig-zag stitch along the edges so they won't fray. Wind the ribbons onto Tilda wooden reels. You can find labels for the reels on page 141.

GLASS CANDLE HOLDERS

Glass candle holders make lovely gifts. Here they are decorated with patterned silk paper and paper images. You can find equipment for making candles in craft stores.

ROMANTIC SOAPS

The soaps are made of natural soap paste. You can add colour and fragrance to it, or leave it without additives if the gift is for someone with allergies.

Wrap the soaps in cellophane and then in wrapping paper, parcel paper, fabric or similar. Finally, decorate them with stickers, paper images and embellishments before placing them in a decorated gift box.

Decoration Ideas

CARDBOARD CORNET
Make a cornet using decorated cardboard and glue. Use a quarter of a circle as a pattern for the cornet. Decorate the cornets with 3D stickers and ribbons. Attach a ribbon to use as a hanger with a stapler or brads.

TREE DECORATIONS
Christmas decorations made out of small fluted tartlet tins look best if you can find old tins with some patina on them. Flea markets and garage sales would be a great place to look. If you can't find any, new ones will work as well.

Make a hole by placing the fluted edge of the tartlet tin down on a towel. Press the sharp point of some scissors against the tin until it breaks through. Twist the scissors to enlarge the hole slightly.

Make holes in the paper images using a hole punch and attach string as a hanger.

Make your Christmas
memorable and unique with
distinctive tree decorations

You can enjoy an everlasting
gingerbread house year after year ...

Everlasting Gingerbread House

HOW TO MAKE

You will need to work carefully and accurately to make this house. Read through all the instructions before you begin. Making the window panes can be fiddly, but you can skip this step if you want to. If you do, just glue the windows to the house as they are shown on the pattern. You also won't need to cut openings for the windows or paper the inside of the house.

It is a good idea to use strong, but not too thick, cardboard. The back of a writing pad or the cardboard envelope from large photo paper would be perfect.

WALLS

The pattern for the walls is in three parts: front wall (page 136), side wall (page 137) and back wall (page 136). The front and back walls are marked with a folding edge. Turn the pattern over along the folding edge to make sure you obtain the whole image. You also need two side walls.

Trace the walls onto cardboard and cut out using a utility knife and ruler. Also cut holes for the windows. To make the bay on the front wall, lightly score and then fold along the vertical lines on the pattern.

Place the walls face down next to each other. Glue the touching edges together with strong duct or plastic tape so the walls are connected, but can easily be folded, see figure A.

YOU WILL NEED
Cardboard for walls, roof and floor
Brown fabric for the walls
White fabric for the roof
Double-sided fusible web
Buttons and lace for decorations
Decorated paper for the interior windows and doors (see page 140)

See patterns on pages 135–137.

Cut a strip of fabric slightly larger than the whole pattern. Iron fusible web to the wrong side of the fabric and pull off the paper. Place the fabric on the ironing board with the adhesive side up. Place the strip of wall pieces down on top.

Cut around the walls about 2–3mm (⅛in) from the edge. Cut a notch by every corner. Fold the fabric towards the back of the walls and iron carefully. The fusible web will act as an adhesive, see figure B. Be careful not to tighten the fabric too much so you can still fold the walls. Cut an x-shaped hole in the fabric for each window opening, fold the fabric around the edge and iron, see figure C. Use tape as well if the fusible web isn't strong enough.

A

B

C

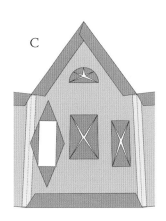

It's a good idea to paper the inside walls with decorated paper if you want to have open windows. Trace the walls onto the paper and cut 2–3mm (⅛in) inside the line so the wallpaper is smaller than the actual walls. Glue the wallpaper to the actual walls, see figure D.

FLOOR

The floor pattern is also marked with a folding edge and should be doubled. Make the floor in the same way as the walls, with fabric and decorative paper.

The slot along the back edge is there to put light inside the house when you are done.

Fold and bend the house so it will fit the floor. The walls are supposed to lean inwards slightly (see picture opposite). Use a glue gun and attach the walls to the floor one at the time. Hold the walls until the adhesive has dried. Also glue together the last two vertical edges, see figure E.

ROOF

The roof pattern is marked with a folding edge and must be doubled. Score along the folding edge so the roof can be folded easily. Cut out a rectangle on the front edge of the roof for the bay as marked with the dotted line. Cover the roof the same way as the walls, but with white fabric.

Glue the roof to the house with the glue gun and make sure the notch in the roof is over the bay, see figure F. The bay pattern should also be doubled, and scored so it can be folded along the folding line. Cover and attach, see figure G.

WINDOWS AND DOOR

You will find the windows and door on page 140. Make copies or scan and print them onto slightly thicker matt photo paper. It's a good idea to have two copies in case you make a mistake. Start to cut out the windows using a utility knife and ruler. Then, if you wish, carefully cut out the window and door panes. Glue the windows and door in place.

Glue buttons onto the roof and lace around the roof edge with a glue gun if you want to decorate the house. Add some glitter glue to the window and door frames.

D

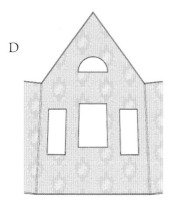

E

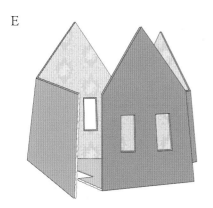

F

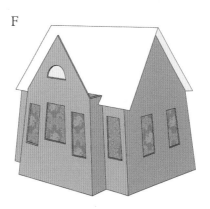

G

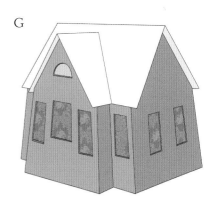

Purse

HOW TO MAKE

Cut a strip measuring 20 × 34cm (8 × 13½in) and a strip measuring 3 × 34cm (1⅛ × 13½in) for the outside of the purse. Cut a strip measuring 22.5 × 34cm (9 × 13½in) for the lining. Also cut a strip measuring 80 × 7cm (31½ × 2¾in) for the ruffle. Add seam allowance to all of the measurements.

Fold under the seam allowances on the short sides of the ruffle. Fold and iron the strip in half lengthwise. Tack (baste) along the open side and gather the ruffle until it is 34cm (13½in) long.

Bond the interfacing to the wrong side of the thin strip for the purse. Place the thin and the wide strips for the outside of the purse right sides together with the ruffle in between, and sew along the edge, see figure A. Sew the lining strip to the raw edge of the thin strip.

YOU WILL NEED
Fabric for the purse
Fabric for the lining
Iron-on fusible interfacing
Ribbon for the strap
Buttons for decorations

Fold the purse and lining right sides together and sew along the open side, see figure B. Refold the purse so that the seam is in the middle and sew the raw edges at the top and bottom closed, leaving an opening in the lining, see figure C.

Turn the purse right sides out and push the lining down into the purse. Iron the purse and then sew closely around the top edge so the lining will stay in place. Attach a ribbon as a carrying strap. Decorate with buttons if you want to.

A

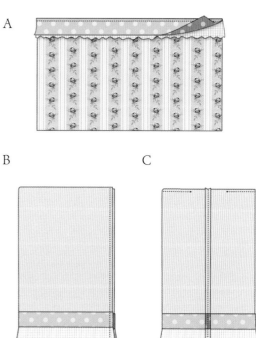

B   C

Red and White Christmas

The kitchen is decorated in red and white and the Christmas workshop has started. Advent calendar gifts are hanging from a wreath above the table so presents can be opened every morning with breakfast.

Presents for friends and family are ready and beautifully wrapped with homemade Christmas cards and notes.

Santa Claus

HOW TO MAKE
Each of the patterns for the body, jacket and pants are divided in two parts. Put the parts together, matching points A and B.

BODY
Cut two pieces of fabric for the skin and two pieces for the hat. Use the pattern to position the parts together along the slanting dotted line, see figure A. Sew the parts for the hat to the body as shown in figure B.

Place the two parts right sides together, trace the pattern and sew around the shape, see figure C. Cut out, turn right sides out and iron the body.

Fold fabric for the arms and legs right sides together. Trace, sew around, cut out, turn right sides out and iron. Fold under the edges on the body and arms. Stuff the pieces. Stitch the opening at the bottom of the body closed.

LEGS, BOOTS AND PANTS
On this Santa the legs should be sewn to the pants before the pants are attached to the body. Notice that the pants pattern is marked with a folding edge and should be doubled. Place the two parts for the pants right sides together, see figure D.

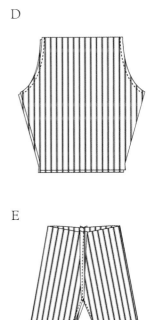

Make the boots, following the instructions for legs on page 98. After you have stuffed them, sew straight stitches across the front seams, using contrast thread, to make the laces.

Fold the pants so the seams lay over each other. Then sew the inside leg seams, see figure E.

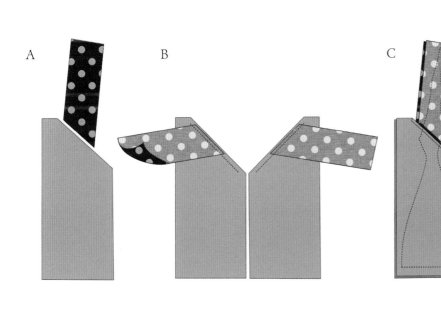

A B C D

E

Turn right sides out, fold the raw edges under and iron the pants. Tack (baste) around each leg opening and place the legs inside the openings to fit. Stitch the legs to the pants.

Cut two strips of fabric for the leg cuffs measuring 5 × 11cm (2 × 4¼in) seam allowance included. Iron under 1cm (³⁄₈in) on each long edge and attach the cuffs around the bottom of the pants, see figure F. Stitch the pants to Santa's waist.

Make the arms, following the instructions on page 98. Then attach them under the neck on each side of the Santa, see figure G.

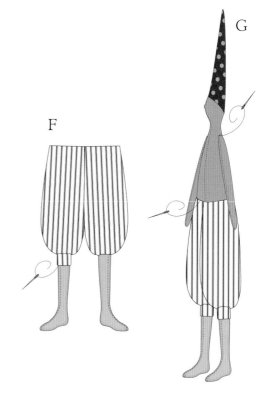

JACKET

Note that the jacket pattern is marked with a folding edge and should be doubled. Cut one piece of fabric using the outer folding edge and another using the inner folding edge, so one of the pieces is wider, see figure H. Fold and sew a tuck in the wider piece for the front buttoned edge so the pieces are the same size, see figure I. Place the two parts right sides together and sew the shoulder seams. Sew on the sleeves as shown in figure J.

Fold up the large seam allowance at the bottom of the jacket right sides together. Trace and stitch around the scalloped edge approximately 2mm (¹⁄₈in) from the fold, see figure K. Cut out the scalloped edge and cut a notch to the seam in between each scallop. Use a wooden stick to turn the scallops out and iron.

You can sew the seam allowance above the scallops if necessary. Fold the jacket right sides together and sew the underarm and side seams on the jacket, see figure L.

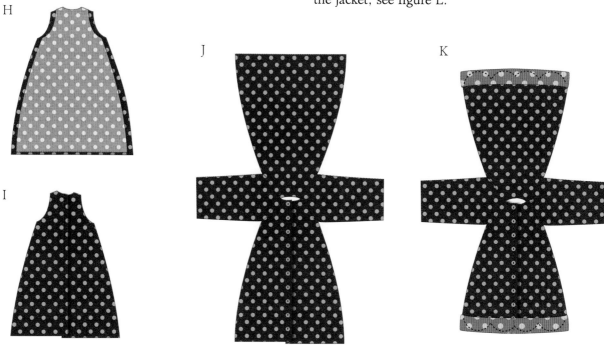

BEARD

Make the face as described on page 99 before you make the beard. Then make a bundle of Tilda hair or similar for a beard by twisting the hair around a small piece of cardboard or something similar measuring about 12cm (4¾in). Thread a piece of hair through the bundle, see figure N. Tie the bundle around the Santa's head and pull the knot up a little to make the beard go around each side of the head, see figure O.

Stitch the top edge of the beard to the head before you cut the bundle at the bottom. If you wish, you can use a glue gun to attach the hair at the bottom.

LOOP

You can sew a loop if you want to hang the Santa. Cut a strip of fabric measuring 5 × 15cm (2 × 6in). Iron under 1cm (³⁄₈in) on each end and iron the strip in half lengthwise. Sew along the open side. Cut a piece of a wide ribbon, long enough to be attached diagonally around the Santa's head.

Stitch the loop to the neck and then the ribbon around the head, see figure P. It is important to attach the ribbon high enough at the front so as not to cover the face and then cross it over at the back of the neck.

Turn out the jacket and iron, see figure M. Dress the Santa in the jacket. The neck opening is quite tight so get a good grip of the hat and pull the head through carefully. Fold under the raw edge around the neck opening and stitch it in place if you want to.

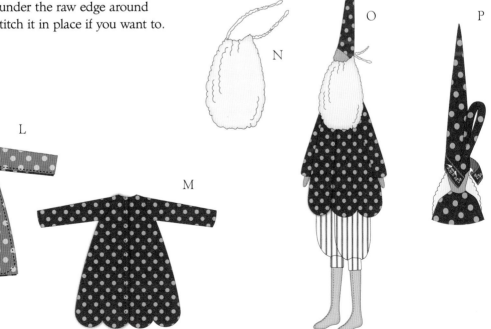

L

M

N

O

P

BAG

Cut a piece of fabric big enough to take the bag pattern twice, adding a seam allowance. Iron under the seam allowance across the top of the bag. Sew a ribbon to the edge if you want to. Fold the bag right sides together and sew around the raw edges.

Turn out and iron the bag. Stuff it with some wadding (batting).

Fold fabric for the candy cane right sides together, trace the shape from the pattern and sew around it. Use a wooden stick or similar to help to turn out and stuff it.

Sew the bunny head as the bunny on page 102. It is not necessary to close the raw edges. Use a glue gun or stitch the bunny to the bag, see figure Q.

Sew frog fastenings or buttons to the jacket (see picture on page 118). Sew or glue the bag under the arm.

Q

Little Santa Girl

HOW TO MAKE

Sew together a strip of hat fabric and a strip of skin fabric. Fold the strip right sides together. Trace the pattern and sew around. Cut, turn out and stuff the body.

Sew the arms, legs and dress in the same way as for the Mini Angel on page 104. Make the hair as described on page 99, but make sure the fringe stops where the hat begins and only attach a little bit of hair underneath the edge of the hat before you attach the hair bundles on each side of the head. Make the face as described on page 99.

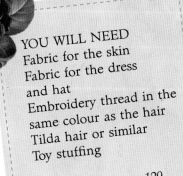

YOU WILL NEED
Fabric for the skin
Fabric for the dress
and hat
Embroidery thread in the
same colour as the hair
Tilda hair or similar
Toy stuffing

See patterns on page 129.

Food Gifts

These are not recipes, but ideas on how to wrap food gifts nicely.

Red and white striped ribbon and gift boxes are beautiful for dark chocolate colours.

A decorated marzipan ring cake is a perfect Christmas present for neighbours and friends.

A pile of macaroon tarts on a cute plate decorated with ribbons can be wrapped in cellophane as a lovely gift.

Homemade (or shop-bought) chocolates would be a great gift wrapped in cellophane paper and ribbon decorations. Place the chocolates in a gift box on a paper doily.

The purse on page 115, sewn in red and white candy colours, and the cornet on page 108 make perfect candy bags.

Angel Stocking

HOW TO MAKE
STOCKING

The pattern is in three parts. Put together the two parts for the foot, matching points A and B. Measure 23cm (9in) up and then trace the stocking top. Draw two lines connecting the top and foot, see figure A.

Cut out two full pieces of the stocking and two matching pieces of wadding (batting). Add more than enough seam allowance on all edges, avoid cutting the scalloped edge and make sure you have matching left and right pieces. Then cut out two pieces of lining fabric from the stocking pattern, ending at the broken line. Also cut two contrasting edges from the part of the pattern above the broken line. Pin the wadding (batting) to the wrong side of the stocking fabric. Sew the contrasting edges to the top of the lining edges.

Place the main fabric pieces right sides together with the lining, top edges aligned. Trace and sew along the scalloped edge, see figure B. Cut out the scalloped edge and cut notches in the seam between each scallop. Tweak the scallops back and forth a little so the fabric loosens along the seam.

Open out the stocking parts that are sewn together and place the two pieces right sides together. Fold the scalloped edge towards the wadding (batting). Sew around the stocking, making sure to start and stop at the ends of the scallop seam, see figure B. Also be sure to leave an opening for turning along the back edge of the stocking, see figure C.

Turn right sides out. Use a wooden stick to turn out the scallops. Push the lining into the stocking and fold the contrasting edge down so it is visible. Iron the stocking.

If you are patient, you can quilt the stocking by hand. Place a piece of cardboard inside it to avoid sewing the front and back together. Make a loop the same way as for the Santa (see page 121) and stitch on the inside of the stocking.

YOU WILL NEED
Fabric for the stocking
Fabric for the lining and contrasting edge
Fabric for the wings
Wadding (batting)
Toy stuffing

See patterns on pages 138–139.

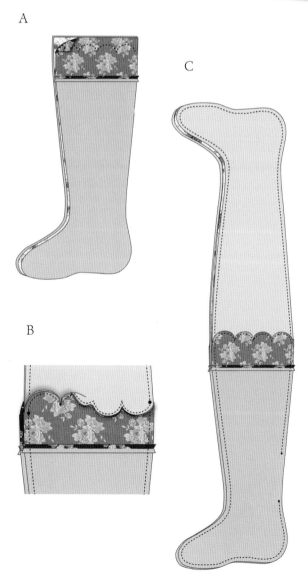

A

B

C

126

Fill your stocking with gifts fit for angels

WINGS

Fold the fabric for the wings right sides together and trace two wings from the pattern. Sew around, see figure D.

Cut, turn out and iron the wings. Sew stitches to match the broken lines on the pattern. Use a wooden stick or similar to stuff the wings. You could press the wings with a flat iron after they have been stuffed. Fold under the raw edges and stitch the wings to the stocking, see figure D.

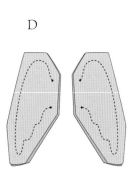

Patterns

Add seam allowances to all patterns unless otherwise stated in the instructions. Broken lines indicate openings, seams or lines for matching the pattern pieces. ES means extra seam allowance and marks openings where it is important to have more than enough seam allowance.

Scan and print out or photocopy the patterns to use. All patterns are shown at actual size and do not need to be enlarged.

MINI ANGEL AND LITTLE SANTA GIRL

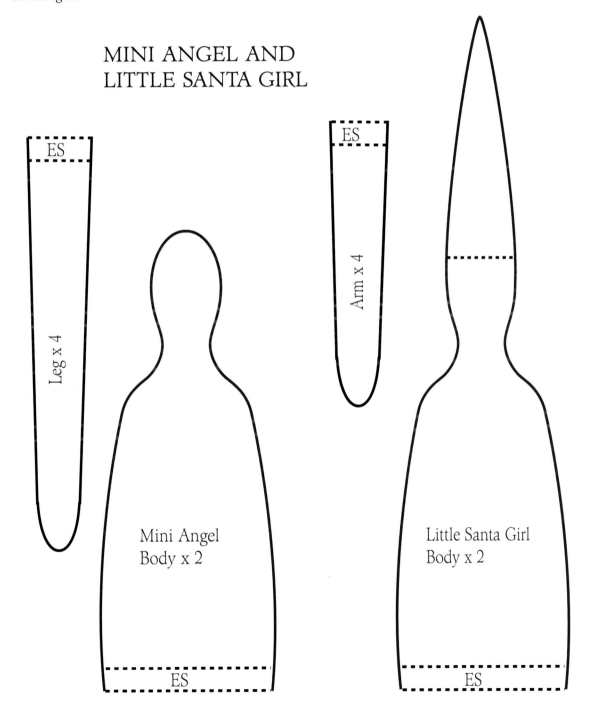

ES

Leg x 4

Mini Angel
Body x 2

ES

ES

Arm x 4

Little Santa Girl
Body x 2

ES

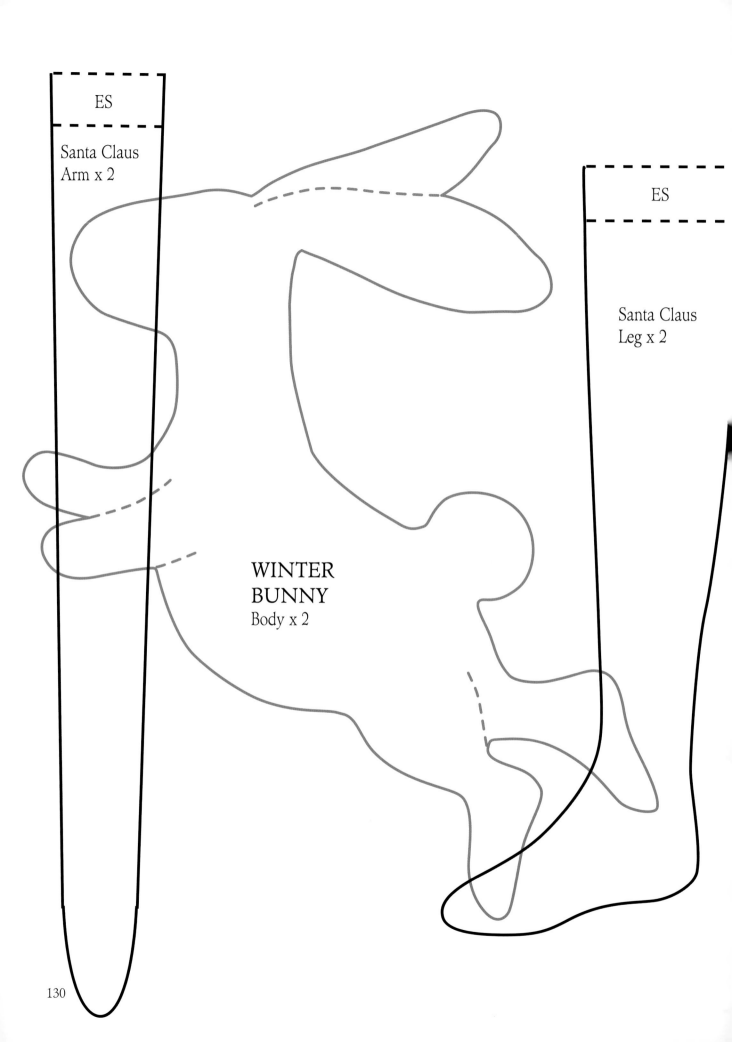

ES

Santa Claus
Arm x 2

ES

Santa Claus
Leg x 2

WINTER
BUNNY
Body x 2

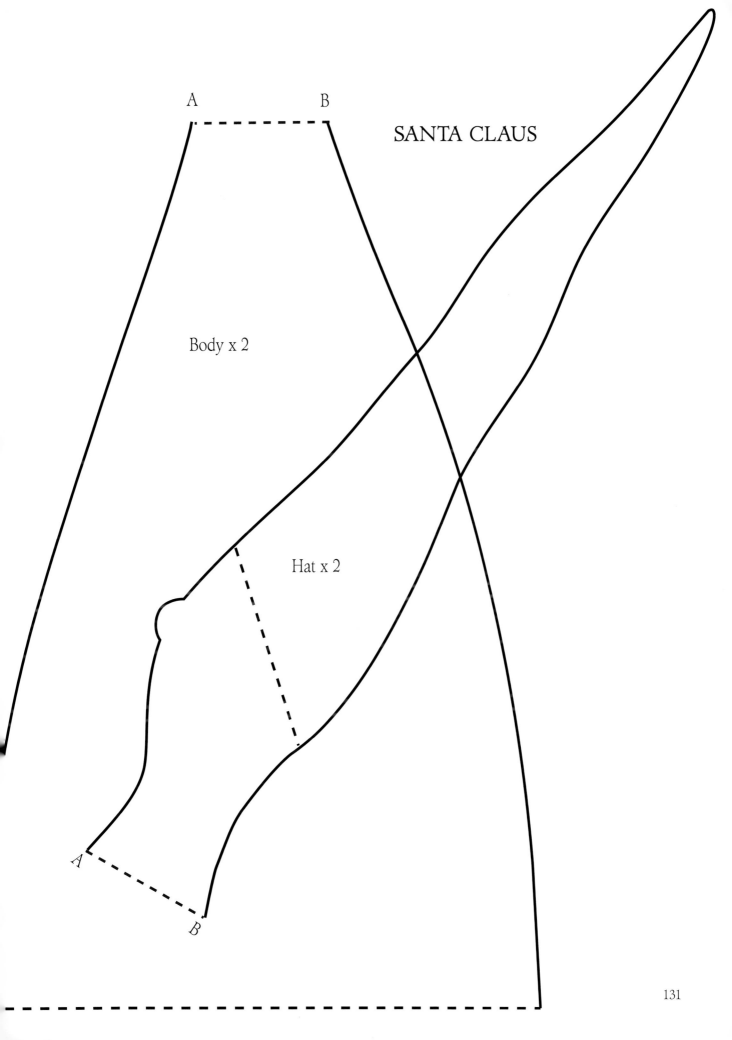

A   B

SANTA CLAUS

Body x 2

Hat x 2

A

B

SANTA CLAUS

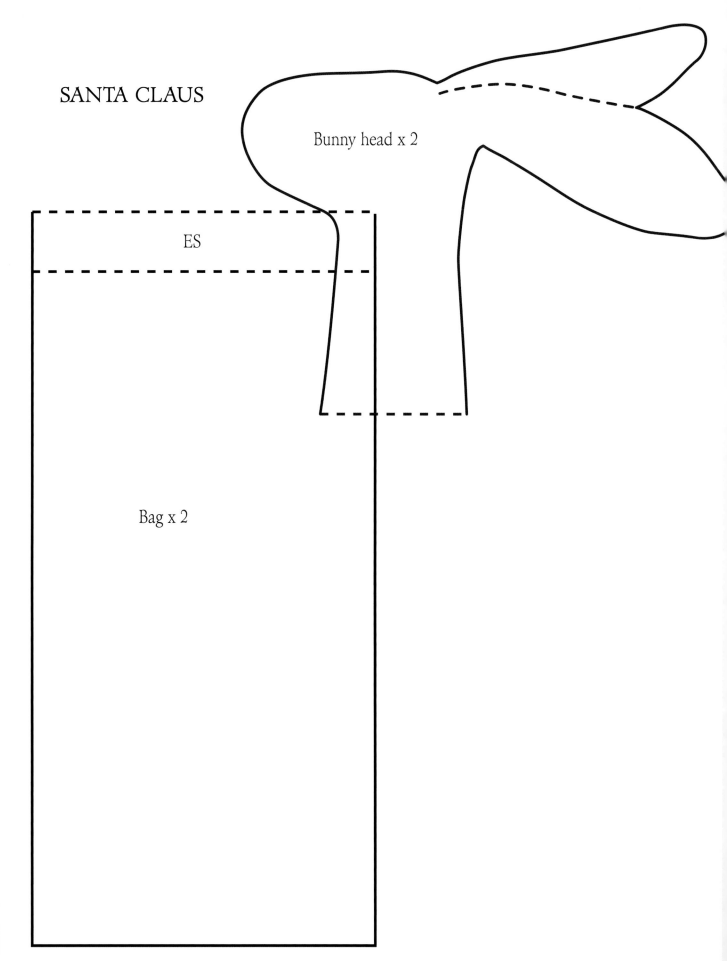

Bunny head x 2

ES

Bag x 2

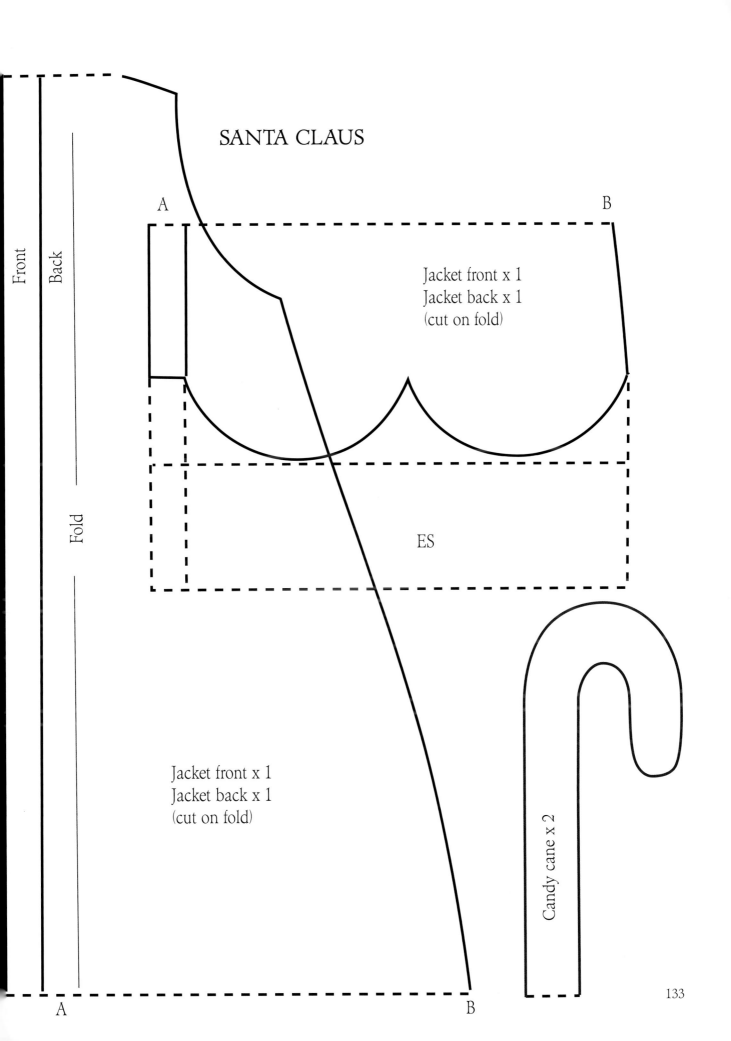

SANTA CLAUS

Front

Back

Fold

A

B

Jacket front x 1
Jacket back x 1
(cut on fold)

ES

Jacket front x 1
Jacket back x 1
(cut on fold)

Candy cane x 2

A

B

133

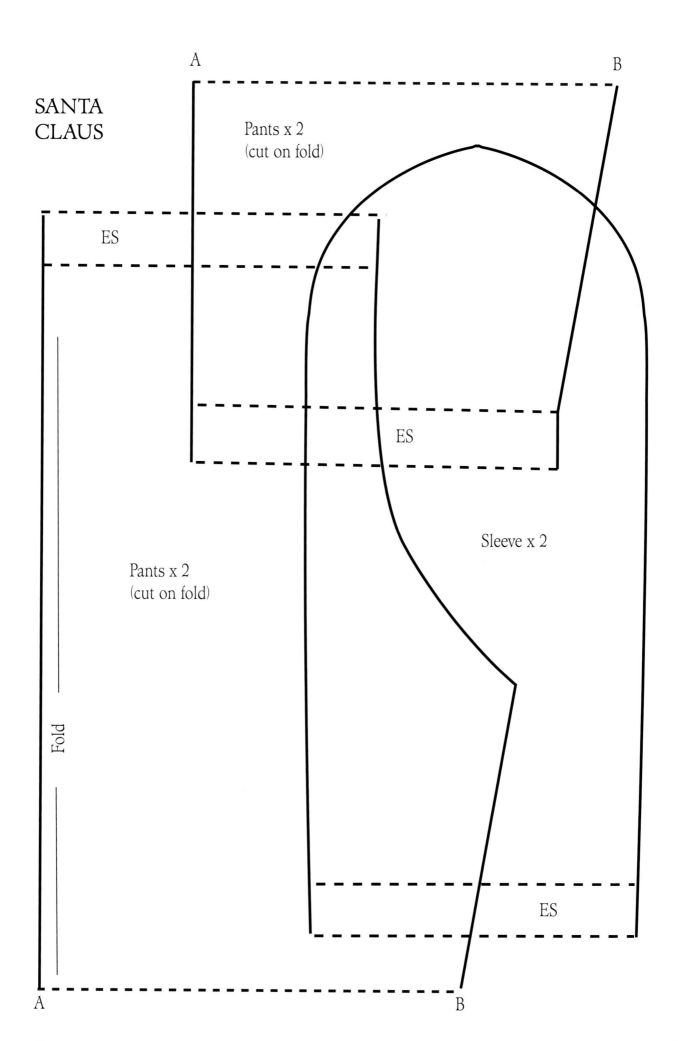

SANTA
CLAUS

A

B

Pants x 2
(cut on fold)

ES

ES

Sleeve x 2

Pants x 2
(cut on fold)

Fold

ES

A

B

GINGERBREAD HOUSE

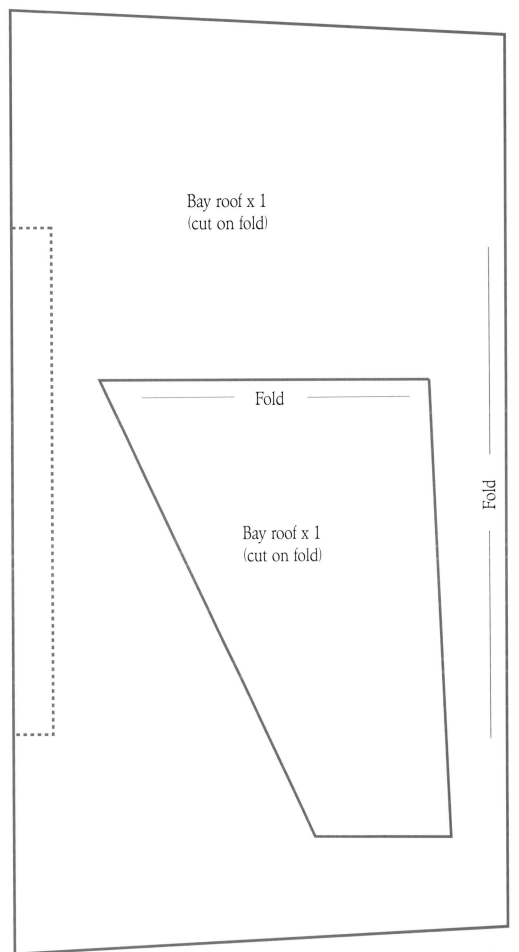

Bay roof x 1
(cut on fold)

Fold

Bay roof x 1
(cut on fold)

Fold

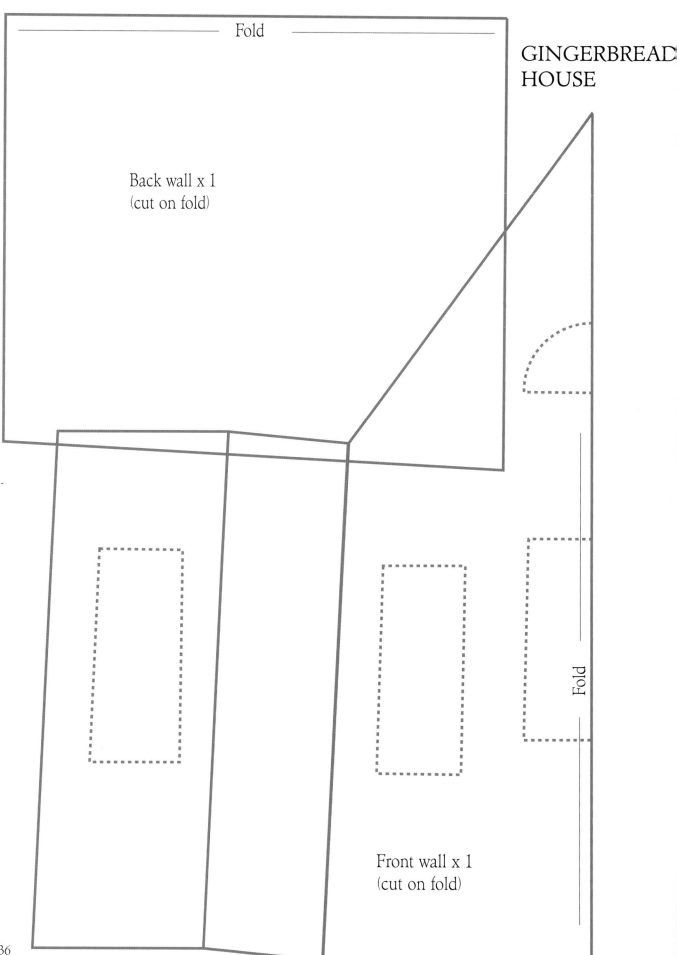

Fold

GINGERBREAD
HOUSE

Back wall x 1
(cut on fold)

Fold

Front wall x 1
(cut on fold)

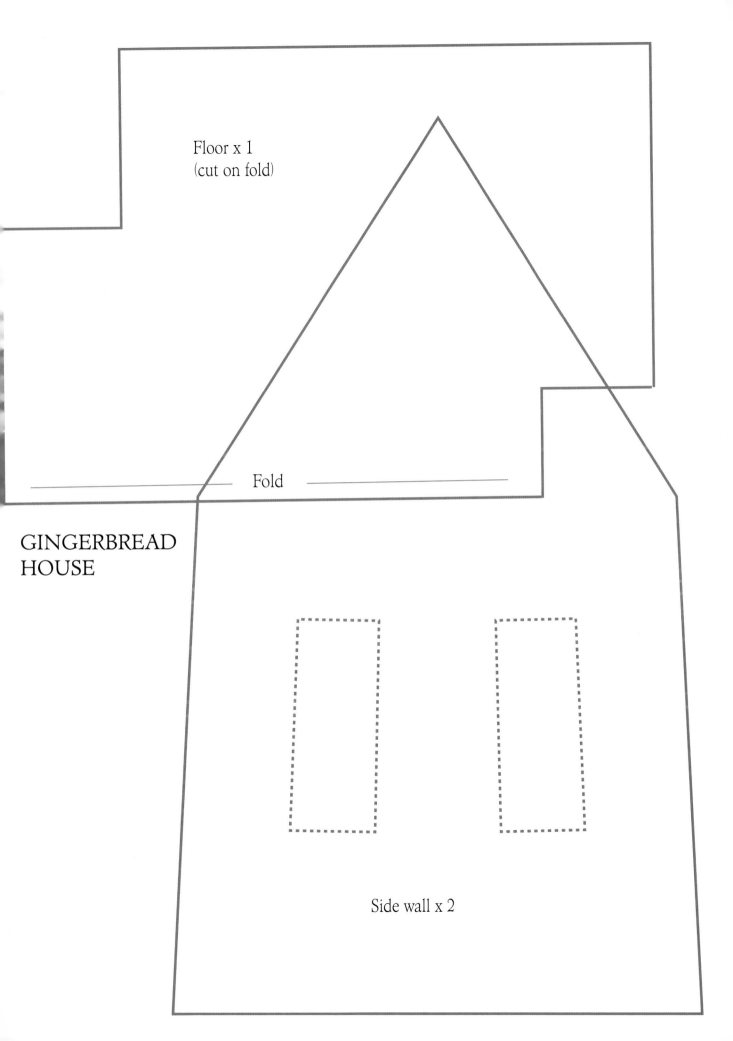

Floor x 1
(cut on fold)

Fold

GINGERBREAD
HOUSE

Side wall x 2

ANGEL STOCKING

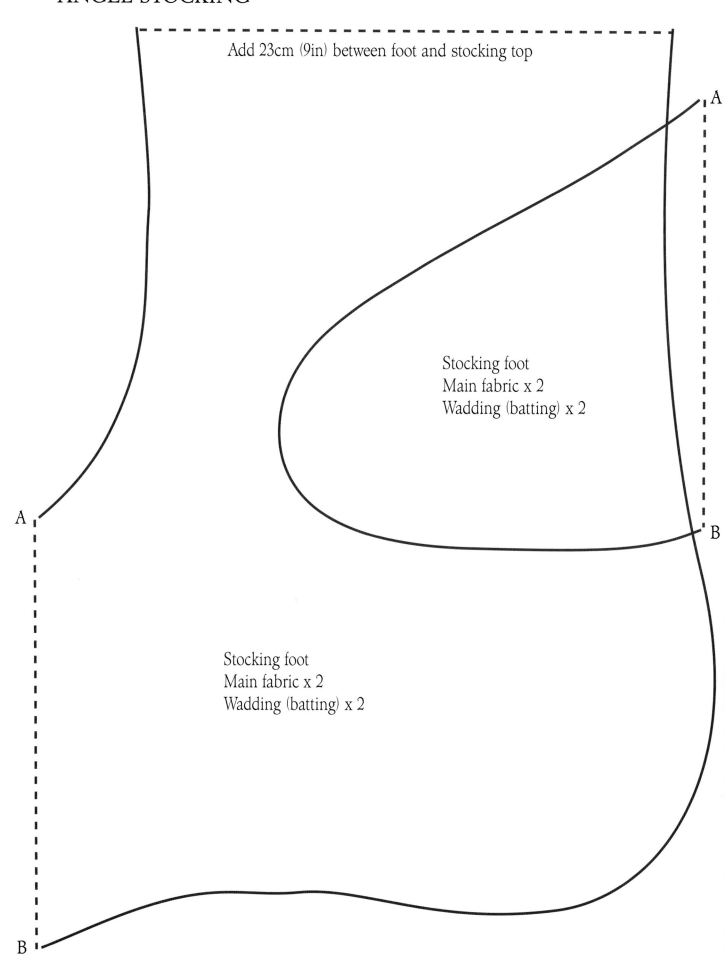

Add 23cm (9in) between foot and stocking top

A

Stocking foot
Main fabric x 2
Wadding (batting) x 2

B

A

Stocking foot
Main fabric x 2
Wadding (batting) x 2

B

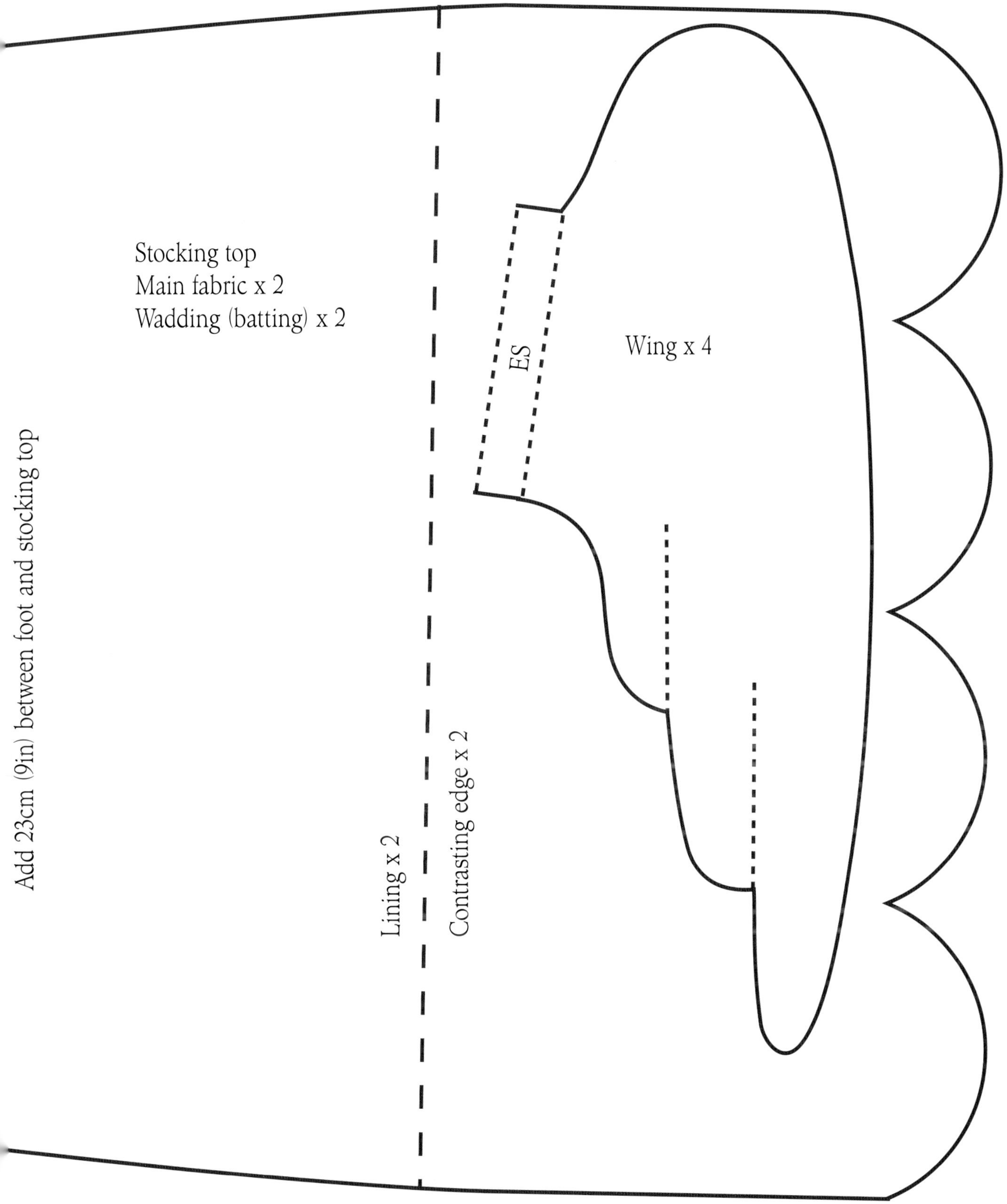

Add 23cm (9in) between foot and stocking top

Stocking top
Main fabric x 2
Wadding (batting) x 2

Lining x 2

Contrasting edge x 2

ES

Wing x 4

ANGEL STOCKING

Accessories

These accessories can be copied using a photocopier, or scanned and printed as decorations for the projects in the book (170–200 gsm matt photo paper is recommended).

Windows and door for the Gingerbread House

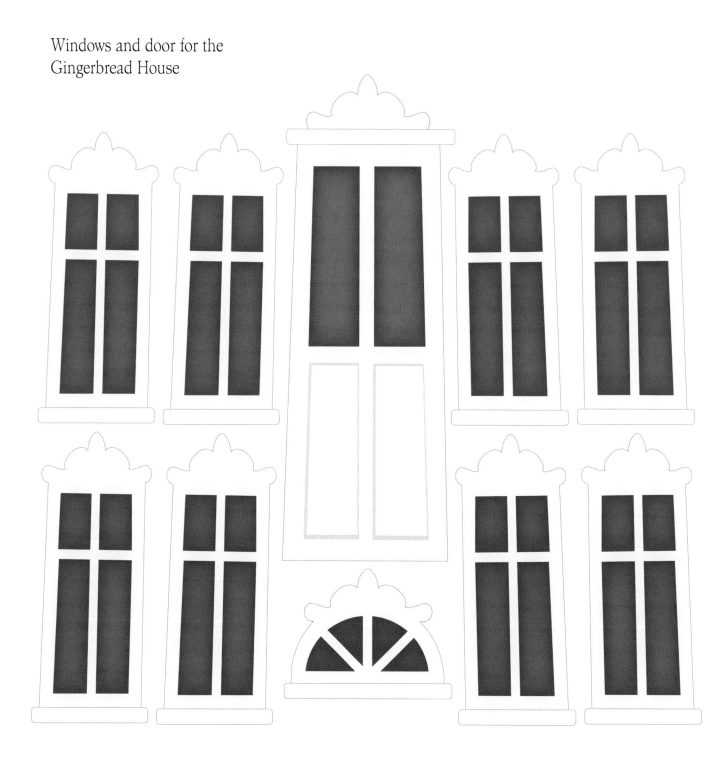

Wings for the Mini Angel

Wooden wheel décor for
the Homemade Ribbons

Wings for the Winter Bunny

Suppliers

Tilda fabric is stocked in many stores worldwide. To find your nearest Tilda retailer, please search online or contact the Tilda wholesaler in your territory. For more information visit: www.tildafabrics.com.

EUROPE

Marienhoffgarden (Spain, Portugal, Germany, Italy, Holland, Belgium, Austria, Luxembourg, Switzerland and Denmark)
Tel: +45 86395515
Email: mail@marienhoff.dk
www.marienhoff.dk

Industrial Textiles (Sweden, Norway, Finland, Iceland, Greenland and Germany)
Tel: +45 48 17 20 55
Email: mail@indutex.dk
www.indutex.dk

Groves (UK)
Tel: +44 (0) 1844 258 080
Email: sales@groves-banks.com
www.grovesltd.co.uk

Panduro Hobby (France)
Tel: +33 04 50 91 26 45
Email: info@panduro.fr
www.tildafrance.com

J. Pujol Maq Conf S.A.
(Spain and Portugal)
Tel: + 34 933 511 611
Email: jmpairo@jpujol.com
www.ideaspatch.com

NORTH AMERICA

Devonstone Square Inc. (USA)
Email: info@devonstone square.com
www.devonstonesquare.com

JN Harper (Canada and USA)
Tel: +1 514 736 3000
Email: info@jnharper.com
www.jnharper.com

ASIA

Sing Mui Heng Ltd.
(Singapore)
Tel: +65 62219209
Email: enquiry@singmuiheng.com
www.smhcraft.com

Mianhexin Trading Co.,Ltd.(FlowerQuilt)
(China Mainland)
Tel: + 86 (510) 87926550
Email: flowerquilt@hotmail.com
www.flowerquilt.cn

Scanjap Incorporated
(Japan, Hong Kong, Indonesia and Thailand)
Tel: +81 3 6272 9451
Email: yk@scanjap.com
www.tildajapan.com

Quilt Friends (Malaysia)
Tel: +60 377 293 110
Email: quilt_friends@outlook.com
www.quiltfriends.net

M&S Solution (South Korea)
Tel: +82 (2) 3446 7650
Email: godsky0001@gmail.com

Long Teh Trading Co. Ltd.
(Taiwan)
Tel: +886 4 2247 7711
Email: longteh.quilt@gmail.com
www.patchworklife.com.tw

AUSTRALIA

Two Green Zebras
(Australia and New Zealand)
Tel: +61 (0) 2 9553 7201
Email: sales@twogreenzebras.com
www.twogreenzebras.com

AFRICA

Barrosa Trading Trust
(Liefielove) (South Africa)
Tel: +27 (0) 847 575 177
Email: liefielove11@gmail.com
www.liefielove.co.za

About the Author

Tone Finnanger is a talented designer and an expert in drawing and painting techniques. She worked as an interior designer and decorator in Oslo, Norway, before moving to a small island near Tønsberg. She has a distinctive style that has proven to be popular with crafters of all ages and abilities.

Tone formed the Tilda brand in 1999 when she was just 25 years old. It is now well known for its whimsical, comical and naive characters in the form of animals and dolls. The brand has also developed a range of craft products for sewing and papercraft that are produced and distributed by Panduro Hobby.

Tone has written several best-selling needlecraft books, including *Crafting Springtime Gifts*, *Crafting Christmas Gifts*, *Sew Pretty Homestyle*, *Sew Pretty Christmas Homestyle*, *Sew Sunny Homestyle*, *Crafting Tilda's Friends*, *Tilda's Christmas Ideas*, *Tilda's Studio*, *Tilda's Fairy Tale Wonderland*, *Tilda's Seaside Ideas*, *Tilda's Winter Delights*, *Tilda Homemade & Happy* and *Tilda's Toy Box*.

Index

A SEWANDSO BOOK
© CAPPELEN DAMM AS and PANDURO HOBBY 2017

SewandSo is an imprint of F&W Media International, Ltd
Pynes Hill Court, Pynes Hill, Exeter, EX2 5AZ, UK

F&W Media International, Ltd is a subsidiary of F+W Media, Inc
10151 Carver Road, Suite #200, Blue Ash, OH 45242, USA

First published in the UK and USA in 2017

Originally published as *Tildas Varideer, Tildas Sommarideer* and *Tildas Juleverksted*

Previously published in the UK and USA as *Tilda's Spring Ideas* (2012), *Tilda's Summer Ideas* (2010) and *Tilda's Winter Ideas* (2011)

A catalogue record for this book is available from the British Library.

ISBN-13: 978-1-4463-0668-0 paperback
SRN: R6349 paperback

Printed in China by RR Donnelley for:
F&W Media International, Ltd
Pynes Hill Court, Pynes Hill, Exeter, EX2 5AZ, UK

10 9 8 7 6 5 4 3

Illustrations: Tone Finnanger
Photography: Sølvi Dos Santos and Ragnar Hartvig
Styling: Ingrid Skaansar
Book design: Tone Finnanger

F&W Media publishes high quality books on a wide range of subjects. For more great book ideas visit: **www.sewandso.co.uk**

Props

LandRomAntikk
www.landromantikk.no

Tornerose
www.tornerose.as

Mowe interiør
www.moweinterior.no

Home and Cottage
www.homeandcottage.no

Acknowledgments

Sølvi Dos Santos for her great pictures
Ingrid Skansaar for beautiful styling
Tom Undhjem for repro

Karin Mundal and Cappelen Damm